LIVE QUESTIONS

IN

PSYCHOLOGY AND METAPHYSICS.

SIX LECTURES

Selected from those delivered to the Classes in
Cornell University,

BY PROFESSOR W. D. WILSON.

NEW YORK:
D. APPLETON AND COMPANY.

ITHACA:
ANDRUS, McCHAIN & COMPANY,
1877.

CONTENTS.

LECTURE I.

SENSATION.

[PREFATORY NOTE.—These Lectures occur in the Courses on Psychology and Metaphysics with the History of Philosophy. As they are intended chiefly for the use of the students in my classes, and for distribution among private friends, and persons specially interested in such subjects, they are printed as they were written for delivery; the first three occur in the Course of Lectures on Psychology; the last three are the conclusion of the Course on the History of Philosophy.]

Good definitions are the best part of any science, and without them there is no accuracy or scientific comprehension anywhere.

It seems to me that there are just now several subjects in the department of Psychology, which are especially in need of somebody's services in this line.

I propose in the following Lectures to do what I can to aid the cause of science, and the cause of religion and good morals also, in so far as they depend upon these subjects, by an effort at a more clear and satisfactory explanation of some of these fundamental facts and phenomena, than I have yet anywhere met with in the books that have fallen under my notice. Among them Sensation is perhaps the first in order.

The two doctrines with regard to Sensation from which I dissent, and to which I wish to call attention in this Lecture, are, (1) that it is a state of the *mind* or soul, and, (2) that it is an *objective* something that can be treated as a concrete reality. The first doctrine is taught, I believe everywhere ; the second has, perhaps, never been avowed or expressly taught by anybody. It is merely assumed in some discussions, and more especially in those with regard to "the transmission of sensations" along the different nerves and to the hemispheres of the brain.

The two doctrines are not necessarily connected. In fact, they sustain a sort of opposition and incompatible contrariety to each other. If we regard a sensation as a mere *state* of the mind, and keep this view in our thoughts, we shall not be likely to speak of it, as being "carried along" the nerves from the organs of sense to the encephalon. In such a juxtaposition of the definition of the word and the statements made concerning the object which it is used to denote, the absurdity becomes too apparent to be seriously maintained. In those cases, however, it is not probable that the fallacy—the mere metonymy of using an abstract term for a concrete one,—has done any real harm to the cause of scientific truth.

There is, however, one case quite distinctly in my mind, in which it seems to me that this assumption has misled a very prominent authority, and through him and his influence, the whole world of thinkers and writers on the physiology of the nervous system.

Some years ago, Dr. Brown-Sequard made a series of experiments for the purpose of testing the, then-received theory "that sensations are conveyed up the posterior column of the spinal cord to the brain." He published an account of these researches in his "*Lectures on the Physiology and Pathology of the Central Nervous System.* 1860.

Without pretending to give an account of these experiments in detail, or in the order in which he made them, I will speak of them as of two classes. In the one, he severed the posterior column, and applied an irritant to the hinder limb of the animal; the section of the cord having been made quite a distance nearer the head of the animal than the entrance of the nerve which goes from the place where the irritation was applied into the spinal cord. In these cases he found, that "sensations were carried up to the brain" as before the operation, from which he inferred that the sensations are not carried up by the posterior column as had been supposed.

In the next class of cases he severed the gray matter within the cord, and left the posterior column untouched. On applying irritants as before, he found that "the sensations were not carried to the brain"—from which he inferred that the gray matter does "carry the sensations to the brain." Later experiments have led, I believe, to the general adoption of the doctrine that the "sensations are carried up by the posterior part of the central gray column and not by the posterior white column at all."*

---

*It should be noticed, however, that these experiments and the inference from them can be understood as relating only to the sensations of the general subjective-sense—the sensations of pain, etc., which appertain to all the tissues of the body, and not at all to the object-sense of touch—by which we perceive the presence and properties of objects external to the cuticle. Brown-Sequard made no discrimination in his experiments between the two classes of sensations; and my belief is, that all the more recent writers on Physiology do regard the posterior column as the channel and conductor of the tactile sensations to the brain.

Now as proving that "sensations are not carried up by the posterior column," these experiments are conclusive and final. But do they prove that "sensations are carried up" by the gray matter?

It would certainly be pertinent to remark from an ontological point of view, that "sensations" are not *things* that can be *produced* anywhere, and transmitted from one place to another, as we send packages by express, or letters by mail. And yet, Dr. Brown-Sequard's interpretation of his experiments, and his inferences from them, imply this view of their nature. If the question were asked him, I do not, for one moment, suppose, that he would say that he so regarded them at the time, or that he so regards them now. He had, doubtless, been led, unconsciously, into this error, by what the logicians call the fallacy of *figuræ dictionis*. Sensations are spoken of as though they were concrete substantial entities that can be conveyed or transmitted from place to place; and therefore without stopping to consider whether they are so or not, he acquiesced in that view, and proceeded to interpret his experiments accordingly.

However, if this were all I have to say of his experiments it would hardly be worth the while to have said so much. But it seems to me that they point to another theory of sensation, which I am inclined to adopt on other grounds as well as on this.

In any view, Brown-Sequard's interpretation of his experiments assumes that sensations are produced at the distal end of the nerves—at the periphery of the body—and carried up by the afferent nerves to the spinal cord; and thence along up the cord—some part of it—to the brain. But suppose "the sensation is produced"—whatever the expression may mean—*in the spinal cord itself*, and we shall have a very different inference from his experiments.

What I mean can be easily illustrated. We stop at a friend's door and ring the bell. What we do at the door is a "*pull*;" what we produce in the house is a "*ring*" or a noise. Or again : suppose we send an electric current along a copper wire into a piece of platinum ; the platinum not being a good conductor, becomes heated. Now what we "produce" at the electric machine or the battery, is electricity ; and what we "send along" the wire is electricity but when it reaches the platinum it becomes heat. The platinum will not "transmit" the *electricity* at all, as such, nor yet will it "transmit" the heat in the sense we are now using the word. But becoming heated, it will heat anything that is in contact with it ; and will especially "conduct the heat" into any substance with which it may be connected at the end opposite to that at which the electricity is "conducted" into it.

Now suppose we have an irritation produced in any sensory tissue in which afferent nerves terminate :—this answers to the battery or electric machine. The current is conducted along the afferent nerves,—which answer to the copper wire in the electric experiment referred to, and whenever it reaches the nerve cells in the gray matter of the spinal cord, they are set into a state of unusual activity, which we may call a sensation: this coincides with the heat of the platinum. The case of the electricity being converted into heat is not an argument. It is neither claimed nor used as such. It is merely an illustration of what I mean, and as an illustration it seems to me to be particularly good.

And it corresponds exactly with Brown-Sequard's experiment. When the white fibres of the posterior column were severed, this fact could make no difference with the sensation if we only admit that the sensation was a state of the nerve cells in the gray matter; for the afferent nerves had entered that portion of the cord below the section, and had produced their appropriate effect independently of it. But when he severed the gray matter he produced a paralysis of that portion of it, which was below the section; and if the irritation was converted into sensation *below* the section, as I believe and think I shall show that it was, no evidence of the fact could have been found in the brain or in any part of the spinal cord above the place where the section was made. Nerve influence, whatever it may be, is in this respect unlike heat and electricity; it will not pass over a section of the connecting nerve, how closely so ever the two ends may be kept together.

Other experiments have shown that if the section be made below the entrance of the afferent nerves into the cord, the effect is produced in the brain as though no such division had been made.

I have said that I think that sensation was produced in that part of the cord which was below the section of the gray matter. And whether I am right or not will depend upon the question whether my view and my definition of sensation are accepted or not. The proof that "something was produced" is found in the fact that reflex action resulted in the limb, when the irritation was produced. The irritation passed up, as we will suppose, to the gray matter of the cord, was converted into sensation by it, was returned as emotion, along the efferent nerves, until, reaching the appropriate muscles, it produced, in them contraction. Just as in the example proposed for illustration; the electricity that passed along the copper wire became heat in the platinum. And it might have been converted into motion or into magnetism, by passing into some other substance. At any rate, the motion in the limb of the animal does occur as the result of the irritation, even when the cord has been completely severed—both parts of it—gray and white matter alike. And with the view of sensation, which I propose for consideration, we have here proof of sensation in the spinal cord when no consciousness of it reaches the brain.

I have already remarked that sensation is regarded by all psychologists, and physiologists as well, so far as I know, as a *state of the mind.*

I cite the definition given by President Porter in his work on the "Human Intellect," p. 128, as being one of the latest authorities I have seen, and equal in importance to any. He says, "*Sensation proper* or the emotional element, comes first in or-"der. This does not occur alone or in part. Pure sensation "is simply an ideal or imaginary experience. Its nature can "be determined only by laying out of view certain character-"istics which always attend it. Though sensation always oc-"curs with preception, it may be clearly distinguished frum it. "Sensation thus considered is *a subjective expression of the soul,* "*as animating an extended sensorium, usually more or less pleasur-*"*able or painful and always occasioned by some excitement of the* "*organism.*"

This definition is given in Dr. Porter's words, the italics being his own also. It makes sensation to be an experience or state *of the soul.* I wish I could find as clear a statement of what is understood by perception. I have looked Dr. Porter's work through in vain for it. And I think I should surely find it in his book if anywhere. The two—sensation and perception—are most intimately connected. They seem, sometimes at least, to be one and the same thing under two different names. But Dr. Porter does not anywhere, as I can find, clearly and formally define perception, or point at all sharply, the difference between it and sensation. He says, "We inquire of consciousness, What is the physical act or "state, [perception]? She replies, It is a process complex in "its nature, but instantaneous in time. It is complex, be-"cause the soul in its single act, discovers two objects—its own "condition" [which is I suppose the sensation] "and some "material reality" [the discovering of which I suppose is the "act of perception.] "One of these is subjective, and hence "is called *subject-object;* the other is objective and is denomi-"nated an *object-object*"—[that is, we have two objects, one "lying within us and the other without.] "One element is "called *sensation* or *sensation proper;* the other is called *percep-"tion* or *perception proper.* The one of these is an element invol-"ving feeling—the other is intellectual, being an act of knowl-"edge. Each requires the other. Each is the attendant of "the other, there can be no perception without sensation, nor "can sensation occur without perception." p. 127. Again on p. 131, he says, of "*perception* or perception proper"—"this, "as has already been explained, is no separate act or state "of the soul; it is only a separable or distinguishable element "of a single complex act. Perception as such is (1.) clearly "and distinctly an act of objective knowledge. (2.) This "knowledge is objective—i. e., the soul not only knows the "object to be, but it knows that it is not itself. . . . (3.) "The object in perception proper is not only known as the "non-ego, but it is known as extended."

And yet after all I cannot help wishing that the Doctor had told us as clearly and as precisely what perception is as he has told us what he regards as sensation.

I turn to other authors, and have consulted them in great numbers, but with no better success. Are the two then, sensation and perception, really two distinct and separate acts? Or are they two distinct and separate or even separable "elements" of the same act, "a complex act?" Or are they only one and the same act, regarded from different points of view—mere alternate conceptions of one and the same thing? If either were really the case, I can see no reason why we might not have them well and clearly defined, and all scholars acquiescing in the definition. But so far from this, I have not been able to find anywhere any such clear definition or distinction of the two acts—as two distinct acts—two elements of one complex act, or even as two alternate conceptions of one single and simple act.

Descartes says, *Princ. Philosoph.*, P. I, § 22: "All the "modes of thinking which we experience in ourselves may be "referred to two general kinds of which one is perception and "the other volition—for to feel ("*sentire*") to imagine and to "understand, are only so many ways or modes of perceiving; "and to desire, to be averse to, to affirm, to deny, and to doubt "are only diverse modes of volition ("*volendi.*")

Locke says, (*Understanding* B, II, c. 6,) "the two principal "actions of the mind, are these two, *perception* or *thinking* and "*volition* or *willing*."

Dr. Reid, however, thought it advisable to restrict the word "perception" to a narrower meaning. "Perception," he says, "is most properly applied to the evidence which we have of "external objects by our senses"—(*Int. Powers, Ess.* II, chap. I,) "the perception of external objects by our senses," he says, "is an operation of the mind of a peculiar nature, and ought "to have a name appropriated to it. It has so in all languages. "And in English I know of no word more proper to express "this act of the mind than perception. Seeing, hearing, "smelling, tasting and touching or feeling are words that express the operations proper to each sense—perceiving expresses that which is common to them all."

This is very clear and satisfactory. But if one attempts to keep in mind what has been said about sensation, while he reads it, he is apt to wonder what becomes of sensation, what room, or place, or function there is left for it. What is ascribed to perception seems to cover the whole ground and exhaust the whole subject.

But I believe that Reid succeeded in limiting the use of the word perception to the narrower sphere which he seems to have intended. Kant and the Germans generally have certainly followed Reid and adopted his views in this respect.

Sir William Hamilton, who by his profession as a logician, ought to be particularly good at definitions and clear in his statements, is hardly more satisfactory in this respect; although he is rather severe and unsparing in his criticisms on others. He quotes Reid apparently with approval, when he says: "Neither ought we to expect that the sensation and its corresponding perception should be distinguished in common language. Language is made to serve the purposes of ordinary conversation, and we have no reason to expect that it should make distinctions that are not of common use," etc. (*Lects. on Metaphysics, Lect. XXIV.*)

But in attempting to improve on what he found done to his hand, he says, Lect. XXIV. "It ought, therefore, in the first place, to have been noticed that the genuine phenomena of knowledge and feeling are always found cöexistent and yet always distinct." . . . Perception proper is the consciousness, through the senses, of the qualities of an object known as different from self; Sensation proper is the con-

"sciousness of the subjective affections, of pleasure, or pain, "which accompanies that act of knowledge."

This language is modified by Hamilton's peculiar theory of consciousness—with which, however, we are not now concerned. Translating the thought from his vocabulary and peculiarities of idiom, into common English, I think there can be no doubt that he intends to regard both sensation and perception as acts or states of the mind—acts and states of which we are conscious—by means of which we cognize, think of, and acquire a knowledge about such things in the external world as have sensible properties. At any rate he says, "the opposition "of Perception and Sensation is true. . . . Perception is "only a special kind of knowledge, and sensation is only a "special kind of feeling, and *Knowledge* and *Feeling* . . . "are two out of the three great classes into which we primarily "divided the phenomena of mind, *Conation* being the third." Sir William cannot be supposed therefore to have regarded sensation as anything else than a state or act of mind.

Coleridge has somewhere said, I think, that sensation and perception are but one and the same thing regarded from different points of view. If we consider the mental state as produced by an external object, it is regarded and called a sensation ; if as an act of the mind by which we become cognizant of external objects, we call it a perception.

However, I think that most writers agree with Dr. Porter, or rather that he represents their views, in considering sensation and perception as two distinct acts or states, or at least as two distinct elements of an "single complex act."

But they all agree in regarding them as acts or states *of the mind* or *soul,* and no one of them, so far as I have been able to discern, has succeeded in giving a definition to both acts or elements of acts, that makes it at all clear what they mean—by the two words sensation and perception—what is the real difference between the two things, or whether in fact there are two things at all, or only, as Coleridge suggested, one thing considered from two different points of view.

And yet this certainly is a very important matter—important not only in a theoretical point of view—but important also for a clear comprehension of what we mean when we read or speak of sensation or perception. It is important in a practical point also. I have already discussed a case in which a most eminent Physiologist was misled in the interpretation of some exceedingly valuable experiments that he had made with great pains and skill, by the want of a clear conception of what is meant by the word sensation. In that case he had unconsciously accepted—or rather acquiesced in, a view which nobody would accept when attention is directly called to it.

I will now introduce another case in which a man, equally eminent as a Naturalist, has made, as I think, an equally obvious mistake, in interpreting another class of phenomena in consequence of the same want of a clear notion of what perception is, and how it differs, if indeed it differs at all, from sensation.

In the number of *Appleton's Popular Science Monthly*, for Oct., 1874, Professor Huxley contributed an exceedingly interesting article on the question "*Are Animals* Automatons." I think I should write the word "*Automata.*" But never mind that. I agree with the author entirely, in his general conclusion; although I should explain the matter in different words; I should also, object to the scope which he gives to the word "animals" in his discussion. Huxley introduces the case of a frog, from which had been taken away "all that part of the brain which we call hemispheres." He says, "If that operation is properly performed, very quickly and very skillfully, "the frog may be kept in a state of full bodily vigor for "months, or it may be for years, *but it will sit forever in the "same spot. It sees nothing, it hears nothing.* It will starve "sooner than feed itself, although if food is put into its mouth, "it swallows it. On irriation it jumps or walks, if thrown "into the water it swims. But the most remarkable thing it "does is this—you put it in the flat of your hand, it sits "there, crouched, perfectly quiet, and would sit there forever. "Then if you incline your hand, doing it very gently and "slowly, so that the frog would naturally tend to slip off, you "feel the creature's fore-paws getting a little slowly on to the "edge of your hand until he can just hold himself there, so "that he does not fall; then, if you turn your hand, he "mounts up *with great care and deliberation*, putting one leg in "front and then another, until he balances himself with per"fect percision upon the edge of your hand. The doing of "all this requires a delicacy of co-ordination, and an adjust"ment of the muscular apparatus of the body, which is only "comparable to a rope-dancer among ourselves—in truth a frog "is an animal very poorly constructed for rope-dancing, and "on the whole we may give him rather more credit than we "should to a human dancer. These movements are performed "with the utmost steadiness and percision, and you may vary "the position of your hand, and the frog, so long as you are "reasonably slow in your movements, will work backward and "forward like a clock. And what is still more remarkable is "this—*that if you put him on a table and put a book between him "and the light, and give him a little jog behind, he will jump— "take a long jump possibly*—BUT HE WON'T JUMP AGAINST THE

"BOOK, he will jump to the right or to the left, but he will get "out of the way, showing that, *although he is absolutely insensi- "ble to ordinary impressions of light, there is still something "which passes through the sensory nerve*, acts upon the machin- "ery of his nervous system, and causes it to adapt itself to the "the proper action." (The italics and small capitals in this whole quotation are my own.)

Now in this account of the frog two declarations are particularly noticeable. They both state, not facts, but inferences or theories ; and are therefore mixed up with a little metaphysics, although claiming to deal only with facts, and mere physical —or physiological science. Huxley says the frog is "*absolutely* "insensible to the ordinary impressions of light." Does this mean that he has no sensations ? or that the book and other objects before him produce none of the phenomena which we call sensations ? Huxley does not use the very word "sensa- "tion." But can his language be understood to mean anything else ? Perhaps he wished to avoid the uncertainty or ambiguity of the word. If so, I appreciate his caution. But he also says of the frog, "it sees nothing, it *hears* nothing." Here I think he can be understood as intending nothing less than a denial of "perception" although he does not use the exact word—*verbum ipsum*—and probably for the same reason as in the other case.

But how then does the frog avoid jumping against the book if he does not "see" it ? If the book produces no "impression" on his optic nerve—so that there is neither "sensation" nor "perception" in the ordinary sense of those words, how does the frog avoid it ? Here is an effect : *the frog avoids the obstacle* before him. He does not *see* "it ;" there is no "perception" of the object. Is it the ordinary reflex action ? That cannot be, unless the book makes an "impression" on the retina, and on the brain as well, through the optic nerve. But it is an effect and must have had a cause. And we have the philosopher resorting to the at present "unknown" and perhaps the unknowable "*something which passes*" through the sensory nerve, etc. But it seems to me that this is unnecessary. He appears to be violating the old maxim—or perhaps I should rather call it an axiom—"entities" are not to be multiplied beyond necessity. I think this "something which passes" is clearly an entity *praeter necessitatem*, and the philosopher is making or inventing a something,—an entity of which we know nothing else; for which we have no other use than to explain this phenomena of a frog without the hemispheres of the brain, avoiding an object which is directly before him, when moving towards it.

Now, laying aside the old notion of sensation being in any sense an act or state of the *mind* or soul, we shall have simply a case of reflex action. The book affects the retina of the eye; the motion extends to the optic lobes—perhaps to the *thalami and corpora striata*—perhaps to the *tuber annulare*: it certainly does not reach the hemispheres *in this case*, because as we are expressly informed they had been removed—and then down the *medulla oblongata* and spinal cord; and from that centre it goes, as an emotion, along the efferent nerves to the muscles called into requisition by that modification of the act of jumping indicated by the statement that he turned aside so as not to hit the obstacle before him. The jump itself was undoubtedly caused by "the little jog behind": and the jump was a reflex act, as I suppose no one will doubt. It was of the excito-motor kind. "The getting out of the way" was, I think, as clearly, a reflex act also, of the sensori-motor kind, caused by the "impression" made by the obstacle on the retina of the eye.

Well why not? If a sensation is a state "of *the mind*"—the frog cannot be supposed, under such circumstances, if indeed, he can be supposed under any circumstances, to have any mind. If sensation and perception are inseperable—whether one and the same act, two elements or indeed two phases, of the same act, I suppose that we must admit that, in this case, there was no "perception" of the book, in the ordinary sense of that word—and so, if no perception, no sensation. And without sensation it could not be a case of reflex action—of the sensori-motor kind—whatever else it may have been. Hence our philosopher's difficulty. Hence too, the resort to that most unphilosophical and most mischievous of all resources—supposing a cause when there was no necessity for it, when one abundantly adequate and applicable was at hand. It was an accepted view or theory of sensation that *misled* him, shall I say? or at any rate it was his view of the nature of sensation that caused his perplexity and led to the suggestion of the existence of some, as yet unknown and unsuspected, substance existing in the material world, exerting its mysterious influences, one, which it will hereafter most intensely interest and behoove all men, ambitious to serve the cause of science and distinguish themselves, to forthwith investigate and describe to an admiring world.

But abandon the old doctrine that sensation is a state of *the mind*—that it is in fact a *mental* or *psychological* phenomenon at all, and all the difficulty disappears; we have at once, clearness, or at least a chance for it, in our conceptions and definitions of both sensation and perception: and had it been done in season we should have saved two of the greatest philosophers of modern times from errors and perplexities—which, to say the least of them, have rendered their services, which are confessedly great—among the greatest that have ever been rendered by any men of whom history anywhere makes mention, far less valuable than they otherwise would have been.*

I propose the simple solution: Sensation and Perception are totally distinct and different, though they are for the most part concurrent and occur at the same time. I would regard sensation not as a state of the mind at all, not at all a mental or a psychical, or a psychological phenomenon, but only a *state of the nerve cells* in some one of the nerve centres, and wholly a physical and a physiological phenomenon. And now the two acts or states, sensation and perception, are distinct, easily distinguished and satisfactorily definable. Sensation is a physical *state* not an act at all; but a state of the nerve cells—an active state doubtless so far as they are concerned. And perception is *an act*—an act of the mind. The one is for the most part produced in us, that is, in some one of our nerve centres, by an external object acting through the organs of sense—as the eye, the ear, the skin, etc. Perception, on the other hand, is a *mental act* which almost invariably occurs whenever any

*I have referred specially to Brown-Sequard and Huxley; but it seems to me that Ferrier, whose work on "*The Functions of the Brain*," is not only the last but the most valuable contribution to our knowledge on these subjects that I have seen, was much in need of the very help I here propose for him and such as he is. All through his work he seems to be puzzled and embarrassed, often at a loss and sometimes misled, by adhering to the old meaning attached to the words "sensation," "consciousness" "volition" and "voluntary action." I shall have occasion to quote his work quite largely hereafter, and the truth of my remark will then become apparent. Accept the definitions and explanations I give and a new light is seen to shine through the whole of his most interesting and instructive work.

outward object produces a sensation; and by that act we become cognizant of the object.

Of course, I do not see how Huxley and others who do not believe there is any mind as distinct or different from the body, can accept this distinction, or the definitions which it renders possible. And I can see no way in which they can escape the difficulties I have alluded to, and in part described, except by abandoning their doctrine with regard to the reality of the mind. Of course, if there is no mind sensation can be no "state of the mind;" it can be only physical, as I regard it. But then if there is no mind, perception can be no *act of the mind,* and can be no more clearly and satisfactorily distinguished from sensation than it has been by the philosophers I have cited, who believe in mind.

Nor do I see how this definition can be accepted by these philosophers who regard the word "mind" as an abstract term and define it accordingly. Herbert Spencer, in one place speaks of the mind as "a phase of nature's order." (*First Principles, Preface.*) Again in his "*Recent Discussions in Science,* pp. 344, 345, 347, he repeats these terms, and with great emphasis, "one's mind is only a series of his own states of "consciousness." Of course a "sensation" cannot be a state "of a phase of nature's order"—or of "a series of states of "consciousness." At all events "perception" can hardly be regarded as *an act* of "a phase" of anything; nor yet of a "series of states."

Two of the greatest authorities in our country, Drs. Flint and Hammond both concur in defining the mind as "a force "produced by nervous action." But manifestly we cannot speak of sensation as a state of any such "force," nor yet of perception as an act of any such nervous action, or of any "force" that may be produced by such action.

Nor do I see how Mill's definition of mind is going to make the matter any better. In his "*Examination of Sir William* "*Hamilton's Philosophy,*" chap. XII, vol. I, p. 253, Am. edition, he defines the Mind as "nothing but the series of our sensa- "tions, to which must now be added our internal feelings, as they actually occur," etc. Replacing the word mind by the definition of it here given, as we have a perfect right to do, and for "sensation is a state of the mind," we have "a sensation is a state of the series of our sensations," etc. The absurdity in this case is apparent.

But for men who like Dr. Porter believe in a mind as something distinct from the body, it seems to me that this distinction will be most welcome.

Nor is there any more reason why Huxley and the men, who, agreeing with him, think there is no mind as distinct from matter, should not accept my definition of sensation—though they cannot, of course, accept the distinction I make between it and perception. In fact, on their ontological theory, sensation *is* what I have described it, just that and nothing else. It can be nothing else than a state of the nerve centres—for they do not admit any mind, of which it can be said to be an act or a state. Sensation therefore can be only a physical or physiological phenomenon. But then, what becomes of perception? I do not see that they can have any use for the word, or any meaning they can attach to it, or any act or state it can be needed to describe.

The question naturally arises therefore, whether we may make this distinction and regard sensation as I have proposed to do, as purely a physiological phenomenon, a mere state of the nerve ganglia?

Now I admit that all the authority of opinion is against me

The theories of many philosophers—perhaps the theories of all the foremost men of the great schools of the day are against me.

And yet the common sense of mankind—wiser in this I think, than the philosophers—is in favor of my view. In our language, and in all languages that I know of, it is the custom to speak of perception as an act, and to say "I perceive;" and to speak of sensation as a state—a state of feeling produced in us by some external object. No language or usage of mankind I think, ever spoke of sensations as produced by ourselves or of perceptions as produced by anything but ourselves. I see not therefore, how it is possible to regard them as but one and the same thing, consistently with this use of language.

But I have a better reason than any I have yet advanced for this change in the use and definition of the term sensation.

When writers began to discuss the matters of sensation, perception, etc., they pursued the psychological method only; they had no other. But the discovery of the phenomena of reflex action—now universally accepted—has changed this whole affair. We have now a physiological method as well, the old writers, pursuing the psychological method, and looking at consciousness alone, could see no good ground to distinguish sensation from perception, as anything more than either two parts of one and the same act or state, at most two aspects of it. They saw as Reid, Hamilton and Porter have so well remarked, that in this act, (if it be only one), there are two elements, which are usually in the inverse proportion to each other. Sometimes, as in ordinary perception with the eye, the emotional part or feeling, is so slight that it does not amount to a pain at all. For the most part it is unnoticed; and we are in fact unconscious of it; so that in reality we assert its existence, if at all, purely and only on theoretic grounds. As a matter of fact, we do not *know* that there is any sensation at all. But in other cases, when for example the eye has become inflamed, the feeling becomes pain ; and the pain is very great, so great in fact sometimes, that we cannot *see* at all ; the intellectual part, the perception proper, disappears. Hence nothing was more natural than the prevailing theory with regard to sensation and perception, and their relations each to the other.

But now the case is different. Take a complex case. Suppose some one should pierce my foot, suddenly, unexpectedly, with a sharp instrument, we know now, that there are three distinct phenomena : (1) an irritation produced in the foot. This irritation extends up to the gray matter of the spinal cord by the afferent nerves leading from the foot to the spine. (2.) The irritation or "*sensation*" extends up to the brain, and then an act of perception takes place. It may be very indistinct—and less distinct than if the sensation or irritation had been less violent. Nevertheless, there is a perception that something has touched my foot, and *I am conscious of the fact.* But (3), there went back from that part of the spinal cord where the afferent nerve entered it, an influence—call it an emotion or what you please—along down the efferent nerves, which produced a contraction of the muscles of the leg and foot ; and motion of the foot ensued—I jerked it away.

In the normal condition of my waking hours I am conscious of all these phenomena, the sensation caused by the wound ; the perception and thinking of it, and of what produced it; and the motion of my foot in consequence of the pain. There might have been one or two elements more, if I had been expecting the act that caused the pain. There might have been an effort on my part to hold my foot still, notwithstanding it, or an effort to resist the tendency to the reflex action. And there might have been too, a consciousness of inability to resist it; if in fact the pain had been so sudden and so great that I could not have done so.

Now, undoubtedly, the irritation in my foot caused a state of activity in the nerve cells of the gray matter of the spinal cord, which did not exist before. Precisely what that was no one knows. And it was *some new state of activity*—one that had been but recently produced, and one which, both extended up to the brain, and excited there perception, consciousness and thought, and which also, extended back downwards, to the foot and produced there muscular contraction and the phenomena of motion.

Shall we then call that new state of nerve-cell activity a *sensation?* and the mental act, the first of three in the order just named, *perception?* That is what I propose.

But the line of proof is not complete unless we take into account the fact that these phenomena of reflex action may be produced, 1st, after the brain has been removed as in the case of the frog, cited from Huxley; 2d, after the head has been entirely removed, carrying with it, of course, the basilar ganglia or corpora striata, medulla oblongata, etc.,—and, 3d, after even the upper part of the spinal cord itself has been removed and the animal has become totally dead.

The question of consciousness in these cases, I reserve to another Lecture. But the phenomena I refer to—which may be found described in abundance in almost any recent work on the physiology of the nervous system—or the chapters devoted to that topic in the more general works—prove, conclusively, that there are several centres from which reflex action may take place, totally independent of each other. Of these the gray matter of the spinal cord, is undoubtedly one. And in this I think that, beyond all question, the reflex actions called excito-motor have their origin. They are caused by any irritation that is intense enough to produce such results in any of the subcutaneous tissues, and in the skin itself, if it be a sensation of pain—and not a mere transient sensation as of warmth or coolness, moisture or dryness. Another of these centres is certainly found in that prolongation of the spinal cord into the skull, which is called by various names as *medulla oblongata; tuber annulare, pons Varolii, optic lobes, optic thalami, corpora striata*, etc. ; that part of the brain, I mean, in which the nerves of the special cephalic or objective senses have their origin as the optic, the olfactory, etc.

Then it is customary to speak of reflex action from the hemispheres of the brain, ideo-motor, reflex actions, to adopt Carpenter's name for them. If this is to be accepted as correct we have a third centre of reflex action in the hemispheres themselves. We know that both the spinal cord and the medulla oblongata may be reached separately—by separate and distinct channels—and that they will re-act independently of the others. And the recent experiments of Fritsch, Hitzig and Ferrier seem to show conclusively, that the hemispheres of the brain may also be reached and excited to action separately from the other portions of the nervous system ; though of course, they can produce the results of reflex action only through the other parts, as means of connecting the hemispheres with the muscles which cause the motion.

It is worth noticing, though I shall not discuss the fact here, that no state of the nerve cells in either of these centres is the occasion of either conscious perception—or of reflex action—*unless it has been recently produced.* Put your hand into warm water, and you feel it at first both as water and as warm ; but in a very short time, you will cease to be able to tell by the feeling alone whether your hand is in the water or not.

Hence I would define sensation as any state of either of the two lower nerve centres, which has been recently produced. And I would add, that in all cases, in man, when the sensation reaches the hemispheres of the brain, there is an act of perception—which is a mental act—and in all cases also there is resulting from the sensation a tendency going outwards which will produce muscular contraction, if the painfulness of the sensation be sufficient to overcome the weight and the inertia of the limb aroused ; and if, furthermore, the tendency is not counteracted by either voluntary effort, or by what is called the inhibitory act of the brain itself.

I do not think that the "recently produced" state of nerve-cell activity, considered as a phenomenon distinct and by itself, has received any name. If it has, the fact has escaped my attention. Here then, we have two facts—a series of most important states or things without a name, and a name, hitherto vaguely used, wandering about without any appropriate use anywhere. Shall we not put them together—marry the two which seem so admirably adapted to each other? I think we had better do it—the union seems to me exceedingly appropriate and desirable.

LECTURE II.

CONSCIOUSNESS.

In a preceding Lecture I have discussed the nature of Sensation, and pointed out what I regard as an erroneous view concerning it—with some of the evils and inconveniences that have resulted from that error.

I propose now to speak of another of those terms, which have been used with a great variety of meanings, and in ways which, as I think, have greatly embarrassed the cause of truth, and the attainment of clear conceptions in regard to some of the most fundamental facts in science. I mean Consciousness. The two are connected—for it has been uniformly held not only that sensation is a state of the mind; but also that it is of necessity, a matter of consciousness.

If we regard sensation as a state of the mind we can hardly fail to make the consciousness of it an essential feature, rather than a mere accidental accompaniment. Even if we do not hold that all mental acts occur within consciousness, we can hardly fail to regard the consciousness of sensations as being so essential to them that we should deny that there had been any sensation if there had been no consciousness of it. And this, I think, is the view that has hitherto been entertained by both psychologists and physiologists.

I cite in this connection only one author, Dr. W. B. Carpenter: and he is eminently worthy of being cited, having been one of the earliest to investigate and describe the phenomena of reflex action. He also gave to actions of that kind the classification and the names which, with few exceptions and modifications, have been retained to the present day. I cite "*Animal* "*Physiology*," § 430, and following, "If, taking the nervous "system of man as the highest type of this apparatus, we an- "alyze in a general way the actions to which it is subservient, "we find that they may be arranged under several distinct groups, "which it is very important to consider apart, whether we are "studying his *psychical* functions of those of the lowest ani- "mals. 1. The simplest mode of its action is that in which "an impression made upon the *afferent* nerve excites, through "the ganglionic centre in which it terminates, an impulse in "the *motor* nerve issuing from it, which, being transmitted by "it to the muscular apparatus calls forth a respondent move- "ment, of this action, which is called *reflex*, or '*excito motor*,' "which may be performed *without any consciousness* (these "italics are my own) either of the impression or of the mo- "tion, we have examples," etc. Here it will be noted, (1.) that he does not speak of a sensation as having been produced at all—nor (2.) of any active state of the nerve cells "in the "centre,"—which, in this case, is the spinal cord—at all; but only of an "impression transmitted" through the ganglionic centre to the muscular apparatus, etc.

But he proceeds, "2. If the ganglionic centre to which the "impression is conveyed, should be one through which the "consciousness is necessarily affected, *sensation* becomes a ne- "cessary link in the circular chain, and the action is distin- "guished as *consensual* or 'sensori motor.' The closing and "opening of the pupil of the eye in accordance with the "amount of light that falls upon the retina—are examples of "this class. In the foregoing operations no *mental* change "higher than simple *consciousness* of *impression*—that is to say, "*Sensation*, with which may be blended the simple feelings of "pleasure and pain—is involved. . . But sensation is the "very lowest form of mental action." Here clearly not only is sensation regarded as a state of the mind, but consciousness is made the indispensable condition and sign of sensation—so that without consciousness of it, no sensation can be recognised or admitted to have taken place.

It will be observed that Carpenter not only does not call the active state of nerve centre from which a reflex action takes place, without consciousness, a sensation; but also that he does not give it any name—or even pay much attention to it.

And yet, undoubtedly, there is such an active state of the nerve cells; and this action is essential to the conversion of the sensation into an emotion, so that the irritation applied to the sensitive surface or tissue, may result in action or motion of the limb affected.

As this will become an important fact a little further on in our discussions, I will pause to say a few words more concerning it here. Each afferent nerve enters some one of the ganglionic nerve centres. From most of these centres there emerge efferent nerves; and in all cases of reflex action, the irritation must pass through one of these centres. And there is no doubt, so far as I know—indeed, I think there can be no doubt—that the nerve cells, are called into activity as a means of the transformation. We cannot connect the end of an afferent with the end of an efferent nerve so as to send the current of nerve influence, which is, in this respect entirely unlike the electric current, through from the one into the other. The current in all cases, goes through the ganglion. Hence, although we do not know precisely what is the agency or efficiency of the nerve cells of the gray matter, there can be no reason to doubt their activity, or the necessity of that activity, to the production of reflex action of any kind.

The above citations from Carpenter would be sufficient for our present purpose, but as in the words I have cited, he has spoken of "several groups" of actions, to which the nervous system *of man* is subservient, I will give his definition of the remaining three. "3. When the outness or externality of "the objects which give rise to our sensations has been recog-"nized by *perception*, we begin to form ideas respecting their "nature, qualities, etc. . . and they (the ideas) may ex-"press themselves in action, as we see in the movements of a "somnambulist. . . This form of nervous activity, which "may be termed *ideo-motor*, seems to be the ordinary mode in "such of the lower animals as are governed by *Intelligence* "rather than by Instinct; but it is abnormal and exceptional in "man." "4. With ideas are associated feelings of various "kinds which constitute *Passions* and *Emotions*, and these, "when strongly excited, may become distinct springs of action, "so powerful as even to master the control of the will, pro-"ducing *emotional* movements. [Carpenter has elsewhere called them *emoto-motor* motions.]

As to the fifth class, he says, "In the well-regulated mind of "man, however, the *Will* possesses supreme direction over the "whole current of thought, feeling and action." This, of course makes the fifth class and completes the list.

But I see no good reason for the fourth class, as distinct from the others. And in the preceeding Lectures [omitted in this publication], I have given my reasons for regarding the spinal cord as the centre of the lowest or *excito-motor* emotions, and the continuation of the spinal cord after it enters the skull—the sensorium, as the centre of the "*sensori-motor;*" and the hemispheres, as the centre of the "ideo-motor" emotions. And I propose also, to make the word "reflex" more general than Carpenter has done, and use it to include all three kinds. And I propose to call the active states of the nerve centres which result in the *excito-motor* and the *sensori-motor* actions—*sensations;* and that in the hemispheres, when regarded from a purely physical point of view, an *idea* or *ideation.*

This excitement in the spinal cord is produced by any condition of the body. The active state of the sensorium is produced by any external object acting through the special or objective senses. And the active state of the brain—which I propose to call an "idea," is produced by either a state of the body or any external object, extending its influence up through the crura cerebrii or the corpus callosum, when there is any, into the hemispheres.

But to return to the subject now more immediately before us—Consciousness. Is consciousness essential to sensation, either as an element or as a sign? I propose to answer this question in the negative. But we must first consider a little what is really meant by consciousness.

Sir William Hamilton says, [*Philosophy of the Conditioned,* p. 57, note,] "The Greeks, perhaps fortunately, had no special "term for consciousness." And at the end of the note he says, "some, however, of the commentators on Aristotle intro-"duced the term Συναίσθησις, employing it by extension "for consciousness in general. The word Συνείδησις, however, certainly occurs—but probably it meant more nearly the same, as our word conscience, rather than consciousness.

Locke, as is well known, referred the origin of all knowledge to *Sensation* and *Reflection*. And in this connection he defines reflection as follows : "The other fountain . . . . "which I call Reflection . . . from which experience "furnisheth the understanding with ideas, is the perception of "the operations of our own mind within us, as it is employed "about the ideas it has got ; which operations, when the soul "comes to reflect on and consider, do furnish the understanding with another set of ideas, which could not be had from "things without—and such are perception, thinking, doubting, believing, reasoning, knowing, willing, and all the different actings of our own minds." (Essay B, II, ch. I, § 4.) And in § 19 he says, "Consciousness is the perception of what "passes in a man's own mind." It is difficult to see how the two words, as thus defined, can be regarded as having a different meaning.

And yet Hamilton, (work before cited p. 53,) says, "Aristotle, Descartes, Locke and philosophers in general, have regarded consciousness, not as a particular faculty, but as the "universal condition of intelligence." Locke does, undoubtedly, argue at great length, and with great pertinacity, that there is no consciousness without thought, and no thought, feeling or will without consciousness. But it does not seem to me, on a careful reading of all that Locke has said, and especially the words just quoted, that Hamilton has quite appreciated what Locke did really mean by the word consciousness.

However it seems worth while to quote Hamilton's words a little further. He says, "Reid on the contrary, following, "probably, Hutcheson, and followed by Stewart, Royer Collard, and others, has classed consciousness as a coördinate "faculty with the other intellectual powers—distinguished from "them, not as a species from the individual, but as the individual from the individual. And as the particular faculties "have each their peculiar object, so the peculiar object of consciousness is, the *operations of the other faculties themselves, to "the exclusion of the objects* about which these operations are "conversant.

Hamilton, as we all know, had a peculiar view of consciousness. It had been held that we have "*immediate*" knowledge of external things. This he was not disposed to deny, though others had denied it, and he sought rather to confirm and justify the doctrine. Hence he says, p. 37, "*Consciousness and "immediate knowledge* are thus terms universally convertible, "and if there be an immediate knowledge of things external, "there is consequently the *consciousness of an outer world.*" Again in his "*Philosophy of Common Sense*," (p. 31, Appleton's edition) he says, "In the act of sensible perception, I am conscious of two things:—*of myself* as the *perceiving subject* and "of an *external reality*, in relation to my sense, as the *object "perceived.* Of the existence of both of these things I am "convinced—because I am conscious of knowing each of "them, not mediately in something else *as represented*, but immediately in itself *as existing.*" Again "*Philosophy of Perception*," (same vol., p. 173,) he says, "the assertion that we "can be conscious of an act of knowledge without being conscious of its object is virtually suicidal."

We see here clearly the motive which led Hamilton to his peculiar theory or doctrine concerning consciousness. Probably no position taken in the domain of philosophy or religion, merely for the sake of any such utilitarian ends, has ever been finally adopted or found tenable. Sir William Hamilton's experiment in that line certainly has fared no better than the thousands of others.

It is due, however, in justice to so distinguished an author and philosopher, to say a word in his defence—not indeed, in defence of his *motives*; for they need no defence—but in regard to the error he had in view. Let us recall a few of his words, and consider one or two of the peculiarities of his phraseology. He says—giving my italics and not his—"I am conscious of "knowing each of them not *mediately in something else, as repre-* "*sented but immediately*," etc. Now the words "as represented," seem to show that he had in mind either the scholastic doctrine of "sensible species," or Locke's doctrine of "idea-images" or perhaps both—both of which, however, have now been exploded. Again the words "not mediately, *in something* else—but immediately *in itself*" look to me, as though he had in mind Hegel's doctrine of "the thing in itself, (*ding an sich*,) as contrasted with Hamilton's doctrine, that we see things only in relation one to another, and as "conditioned." Certainly Hamilton did not mean to say, or at least he would not have intended to say, if only his attention had been called to his assertion, that we perceive external things *immediately*—in reference to the external organs of sense, as the eye, the ear, etc., nor yet in reference to "that state of mind" produced by them, which is called "sensation." It is possible also, that he had in mind Cousin's doctrine concerning the spontaneous and the reflex action of "the Reason," in affirming the existence and reality of external objects.

But admitting, as most assuredly Hamilton did, the use and the necessity of the external organs of sense, he could not have intended to say that the perception of external objects is *im*mediate, as not implying their use.

So too, I think it obvious that he used the word "consciousness" in two entirely different senses. Without being at all aware of any ambiguous middle, he was committing one. When he says, "I am conscious of perceiving," etc., he uses the word in the stricter and narrower sense, as defined by Locke when he said, "Consciousness is the perception of what "passes in a man's own mind." But when he says, "I am "conscious of an external reality," he uses the word in that broader and more comprehensive sense, in which it becomes equivalent, or nearly so, "to perceiving" or even to "knowing," as if he had said "I know immediately, and not as an infer- "ence from a process of reasoning, laboriously and conscious- "ly performed—that there is an external object in relation with "my senses."

Notwithstanding, therefore, this effort of Hamilton's to introduce a new definition for the word "Consciousness," President Porter gives the old and simpler one. "Conscious- "ness," says he, "is briefly defined as the power by which the "soul knows its own acts and states. The soul is aware of the "fleeting and transitory *acts* which it performs; as when it "perceives, remembers, feels and decides. It also knows its "own *states*; as when it is conscious of a continual condition "of intellectual activity, a gay or melancholy mood of feeling, "or a fixed and enduring purpose. Whether the state is in "such cases in fact prolonged, or only repeated by successive "renewals, we need not here inquire; it is sufficient that states "of the soul are distinguished from its acts by their seeming "continuance."

On this definition I have two comments to make.

1. Consciousness is defined as a *power*, "the power by which" —I think this is not quite accurate. Doubtless the phrase might be allowed in ordinary discourse, but in a definition, it seems to me, that not the word "power," but the word "act,"

should have been used. We have been too long accustomed to speak of "mental faculties" and "mental powers" as if they were something concrete, as we speak, in fact, of the organs of the body, as heart, lungs, etc. We have been so long accustomed to this way of speaking, that by a sort of *figuræ dictionis*, we have come to believe that the soul is made up of faculties, as the body is, of organs and tissues. I would say, therefore, that consciousness is *the act* of knowing, or by which we know, etc., and not "the power" or "the faculty," etc.

2. I think that the primary and fundamental ground of distinction between "acts" and "states" is not well presented; and is perhaps rather ignored or winked out of sight. I doubt whether the length and duration of their continuance is the real ground of the distinction. That ground is rather, as I think, the fact that in the one class, "the acts," we are conscious that we ourselves are the agents, the efficient cause of them, and in the other, "the states," we are equally conscious that we are acted upon by something external to and different from ourselves. Perception is an *act*; sensation is a *state*. Of this distinction I shall have occasion to say more hereafter. But I think it of fundamental importance and based upon a difference that cannot be ignored or explained away.

I think then, notwithstanding Hamilton's opinion to the contrary, that Locke did use the word Consciousness in the modern sense, and that this use of it began with him, and is likely to remain.* Hamilton's theory is peculiar, and has led

*There is something peculiar and noteworthy in Locke's manner of introducing the word "Consciousness." In the 4th Section of B. II. ch. I, he used the word "reflection," as we have just seen. But in pursuing his subject, in elaborating and emphasizing his statement, the word "consciousness" comes in only a few pages after the formal use of the word "re-

to forms of expression that are not in accordance with the common sense and the common usages of mankind. And in such conflicts between philosophy and common sense, common sense usually gets the best of it in the end.

On Locke's definition, however, I would offer one or two remarks. He says, "consciousness is the perception of what "passes in a man's own mind."

Note in the first place that he does not call it a "power" or a "faculty" of the mind. I think that in this he was more fortunate than Reid and his followers, including if we may do so, both Sir William Hamilton and President Porter. This use of the words "power" and "faculty" has been, as I believe, the cause of much mischief. Almost instantly, and without thought or consciousness of the act, they have been taken as concrete terms, and set imagination or fancy at work to think what they are—what relation they sustain to the mind, how they work, under what laws, and within what limits they perform their special functions. And the discussions and answers which these questions have elicited have constituted pretty much all that we have been accustomed to get under the head of "Psychology" or "Mental Philosophy."

But they are no concrete terms at all ; when we say the mind has the power of doing so and so, we only mean it is able to do so—we affirm only a property or quality of the mind. We do not necessarily create—and we certainly should not intend

"flection." It seems to come of itself, and as though Locke was not aware that he was doing a thing that was to be forever—introducing an expression that was to take the place of the one he himself had already given out with apparent care and set purpose. But it is so convenient that he himself uses it ever after in his Essay more frequently than the former term and almost to its entire exclusion.

to violate the old axiom and "create an entity *praeter necessitatem.*" It is much the same with the word "faculty." The primary signification of the word was "power," "ability," and then it came to denote the person or body of persons, as in a college or university, who had the power or right to do certain things. But since the time of Reid it has been applied to the mind in a way, which I think has suggested very much the same view of the mind as we have of the body—a heart for one class of functions, lungs for another, and so on. But all of this is wrong and mischievous. Locke's phraseology gives no occasion for this error.

But Locke uses the word "perception," "the perception which we have," etc. I would avoid that word in my definition; both because it is used elsewhere to denote one specific class of the phenomena or acts of which we are conscious, and also because it is so used here as to denote "something that "we have" instead of the act of having it.

I would say then that in the strictest sense of the word, consciousness is the act of knowing what passes in the mind.

The word is also used in several other more general and somewhat different senses, which it is not necessary to discuss here. One of them only, will I mention : the word is often used to denote that which is known by the acts of consciousness ; and sometimes it is used as if to denote a space or sphere within which the facts thus known, occurred.

The practical question now is, what is contained in consciousness ? How much do we know by these acts of consciousness ? Is what we thus know *immediately* known ? And can we be said to know anything else immediately, or in any way except by inference, from what is thus known by consciousness ? Of course, here are more questions than can be answered in one Lecture. I shall therefore confine myself for the present, to one or two of them.

I have already remarked that Locke was very positive on the point that there is no state or act of the mind of which we are not conscious. He says, B. II, c. I, § 10: "I do not say "there is no soul in a man, because he is not sensible of it in "his sleep—but I do say, he cannot think at any time, waking "or sleeping, without being sensible of it. Our being sensi- "ble of it, is not necessary to any thing, but to our thoughts; "and to them it is, and to them it will always be necessary, till "we can think without being conscious of it."

Locke is here attempting to account for "the idea" of personal identity—as derived from "reflection." And it seems to me that all throughout this argument he makes about as sharp a distinction between consciousness and reflection as can well be made. Consciousness, like perception, is an act which we cannot but perform when the conditions which occasion it occur. But reflection has an element of duration in it. It is produced too, in part, at least, by the will directing, controling and guiding it. When a sensation is produced under ordinary circumstances, we cannot but perceive the object that occasioned it, according to the mode and measure of the kind of sensation it produces. So when the mind is called into activity—whether by external objects acting through the organs of sense—by the will rousing the mind to activity—or by the autonomy of the brain, if there be such a thing, we cannot but be conscious that we are perceiving, thinking, willing, etc.; and we may direct our thoughts chiefly to either of two phenomena—our own acts in perceiving, imagining, willing, etc., —or to the object which occasions the perception—or about which the imagination, the thinking, the willing, etc, takes place.

Locke goes on to meet the objection of those who had opposed his theory, by drawing from it the inference, that if the idea of personal identity is derived from reflection—that is from consciousness—men have no existence when they are unconscious, and are not the same persons in any two successive states of conscious existence. And I quote a little farther: "I grant that the soul of a waking man is never without "thought, because it is the condition of being awake, but "whether sleeping without dreaming be not an affection of the "whole man, mind as well as body, may be worth a waking "man's consideration; it being hard to conceive, that anything "should think, and not be conscious of it."

Farther on, § 19, he says, "For they who tell us that the "soul always thinks, do never, that I remember, say that a "man always thinks. Can the soul think and not the man? "or a man think and not be conscious of it? . . If they "say the man thinks always, but is not always conscious of it, "they may as well say his body is extended without having "parts."

Locke's definition and account of sensation is rather peculiar, and ought to be cited. B. 1, c. 1, § 2, defining sensation he says, "Our senses, conversant about particular sensible objects, do convey into the mind several distinct perceptions of "things, . . thus we come by those ideas which we have of "yellow, white, etc., and all those which we call sensible qualities, which, when I say the senses convey into the mind, I "mean, they, from external objects, convey into the mind what "produces there those perceptions. This great source of most "of the ideas we have, depending wholly upon our senses "and directed by them to the understanding, I call SENSATION."

Sensation, therefore, is not, according to Locke, a mere *state of the mind*; it is rather "the source of ideas," the means or channel by which they come into the mind. Again, B. 1, c. 2 § 3. "Thus the perception which actually accompanies, and is an-"nexed to any impression on the body, made by an external "object, being distinct from all other modifications of thinking, "furnishes the mind with a distinct idea, which we call sensa-"tion; which is, as it were, the actual entrance of any idea "into the understanding by the senses—the same idea, when "it again recurs without the operation of the like object on the "external sensory, is remembrance." Here "the furnishing "of the mind with a distinct idea" "the actual entrance of "any idea into the understanding by the senses," he calls a sensation.

Locke lived before the discovery of reflex action, and before attention had been called to the fact of a state of activity in the nervous centres, which may result in reflex action, or in conscious perception, with or without pain—or both reflex action and pain—whenever the irritation produced in any organ of sense or in any sensitive part of the body extends to that centre, along the path of the afferent nerve to the brain. Here, then, we have a phenomenon, now known and admitted by all—of which, however, he knew nothing, to which he gave no thought, and for which he had no occasion for a name. Shall we call it sensation? that is what I propose. And then I shall have departed about as far, perhaps, from the doctrines of this great founder of English metaphysics, as those, who going in the opposite direction, have called it "a state *of the mind*." Locke never went so far as that.

But how about consciousness? I suppose Locke would agree with them that there can be no sensation without consciousness as completely as if he had foreseen and acquiesced in their definition of sensation ; although his definition differs as far from theirs, I think, as mine does.

Believing that sensation is purely a physical phenomenon—a mere state of nerve-cell activity, I do not think that consciousness is any element of sensation ; nor always and necessarily the only sign of its existence.

We certainly know that in many cases of reflex action, from the spinal cord, there is no consciousness of sensation and no perception or knowledge of the muscular contraction, or of the motion of the limb, except what is derived by other senses and is known to the patient himself by precisely the same means as it is known to other persons, and by no other means. A man who is paralyzed in his lower limbs, for example, will often move one of his feet if an irritation is produced on the bottom of it. I suppose there can be no doubt the irritation extends up the afferent nerves, produces a new state of activity in the cells of the gray matter of the spinal cord, and they send down an influence that contracts the muscles and moves the foot. But there is no consciousness of the irritation in the foot, or of the active state of the nerve cells, or of the motion that ensues. If, however, there had been no interruption, the irritation would have, in some way, reached the hemispheres of the brain, and then there would have been perception and consciousness.

But was the active state of the nerve cells in the spinal cord, from which reflex action ensued, or was it not, the same as it would have been if there had been no discontinuity between it and the brain ? No one, of course, knows precisely what it was or is, in either case. No one can tell precisely what are its elements, or in what it consists. But it seems to me that all the indications are that it is the same in both cases ; where there is consciousness, and where there is not. At all events, we know of no difference whatever. And therefore, it seems to me that it is best to call them, for the present at least, by the same name; and to admit that, although consciousness and perception do accompany sensation when the body is in its normal condition, they do not always accompany it and are not, either of them, essential to it.

There is another kindred subject of great importance in this connection. It is what Carpenter has called "*unconscious cere-* "*bration.*" I do not like the name; but it points to, and is used to denote, a class of phenomena that deserve considera-tion.

In his late work "*Principles of Mental Physiology*, p. 515, he introduces the chapter which he heads "Unconscious Cerebra-"tion," thus: "Having thus found reason to conclude that a "large part of our intellectual activity—whether it consists in "reasoning processes, or in the exercise of the imagination—"is essentially *automatic* and may be described in physiological "language as the *reflex action of the cerebrum*, we have next to "consider whether this action may not take place *unconsciously*. "To affirm that the cerebrum may act upon impressions trans-"mitted to it and may elaborate intellectual (?) results such as "we might have attained by the intentional direction of our "minds to the subject, *without any consciousness*, on our parts, "is held by many metaphysicians, more especially in Britain, "to be an altogether untenable and most objectionable doc-"trine. But its affirmation is only the physiological expression "of a doctrine which has been current among the metaphysi-"cians of Germany, from the time of Leibnitz to the present "date, and was systematically expounded by Sir William "Hamilton."

Hamilton, however, would have avoided—and so far as I know he always did avoid—the expression that affirms that "the cerebrum elaborates *intellectual* results"—whether consciously or unconsciously. He always attributed such results not to the brain, but to the mind.

The phenomena referred to are called by others, besides Carpenter, "latent mental modification," or in short, "latent "mental action."

It is not my purpose now to describe at length, the phenomena here spoken of, or to give the proof of their reality. They consist mostly of cases like what occur to all persons. Suppose, for instance, I think of a man now, and cannot recal his name; I may turn my thoughts to something else, and my mind, so far as I am conscious of its activity, may be wholly occupied with something else; and yet, after a few minutes, the name will come to me again; I may go to bed perplexed over an incomprehensible problem, and after a night's sleep, arise with the whole solution as clear as any thought I can have. Or in other cases the solution or comprehension of the subject will not come until after weeks or even months, during which I have been wholly occupied with other things, and have scarcely given a conscious thought to the subject that had thus puzzled me. Carpenter remarks somewhere, if I remember rightly, that nearly all the best thoughts he has ever had, have come to him in this way—weeks or months after he had given up a subject—perplexed with it and disheartened of all hope of ever comprehending it—at some unexpected moment, perhaps in the midst of other forms of intense mental activity, the whole thing would come to him in perfect order, and with the clearness of a long comprehended truth.

How shall we explain these phenomena? Shall we depart

from Locke's doctrine and admit that there are many states or acts of the mind of which we are not conscious? Or shall we admit, as Carpenter clearly claims, that the cerebrum is undergoing, unconsciously, changes which bring it to a state in which the act of memory—the insight into a problem or the solution of its difficulties, is immediate and without apparent or conscious, effort?

I think that the progressing study of the physiology of the nervous system is doing great things for us; and will do even greater things yet. I fully expect that we shall yet admit that the active state of the nerve centres, occasioned by the excitement of any external object, is a sensation—and that it is the only phenomenon that deserves that name. We have then two distinct centres of sensation—the spinal cord, for all the sensations produced by the tissues of the body and their changing conditions, their aches and their pains—and the sensorium, the centre in which all the nerves of the special sense terminate, including, as I think, the sense of touch, regarded as distinct from the general sensibility to pain—as well as the sense of sight.

Then we know also that whenever either of these centres is excited to a state of activity—the state which I am proposing to call a sensation—they communicate with the hemispheres of the brain, the cerebrum, and produce there a state of nerve-cell activity. And what shall we call that state? *With* it there comes perception and consciousness—or consciousness and perception. Sometimes the one and sometimes the other appears, in our after remembrance of the event, to have been first. But what *is* it? Doubtless there is mental activity *with* it. But it is not *mental* activity that we are talking about or inquiring after. To that activity we give the names perception, consciousness, etc. What then shall we call the physical state, the state of the brain—the mere nerve-cell activity—that is associated with it, and which in fact, in these cases, *occasions* the mental states or acts? It would be departing, hardly, if at all, farther from established usage to call it an "*idea*"—or "ideation," than it is to call the nerve-cell activity in the spinal cord and sensorium a "sensation." And there would be an analogy in the two; good reasons, I think for both.

But to our more immediate purpose. We have seen, beyond doubt, that the nerve-cell conditions or states, which we propose to call sensations may take place without our being conscious of them. That they occur is proved by the reflex actions that ensue; that we are unconscious of them is proved by the testimony of all human beings who have been subject to them. Now may not precisely this thing take place in the brain? and may not modifications of its nerve cells be going on when there is no conscious thought—no perception of anything; no consciousness at the time and no memory of it afterwards?

But says the objector, what if we have sensations with no consciousness of them? I answer nothing. We have them and are not conscious of them—that is all. And if we are not conscious of them, they can be no means of knowledge to us—though they may be, and in fact they often are, means of reflex action.

Some changes are going on doubtless, while we are asleep. Not only does the blood continue to circulate, but the brain itself undergoes repair, and is restored to the conditon it was in, before the fatigue and exhaustion that preceded the sleep.

Nor is this all. I have defined sensation as a state of the nerve centres which has been *recently* produced; and I have given examples of cases in which a state that has long continued, ceases to be a means, either of perception or of reflex action. It may be that the nerve cells are never quite at rest in any one of the nerve centres. The keeping up of the vital functions in sleep, would seem to indicate this fact. If so, we have the important modification of our doctrine, that not all the states of the nerve centres can be regarded as sensations. They become such only under certain conditions and circumstances ; and these centers are probably active in the way of sensation, only a small part of the time during one's life.

The idea I have, is easily illustrated by reference to facts (and theories) in physical science. Light and sound consist of different kinds of waves and in different media. But it is only within certain limits that these waves are luminous or sonorous. Light waves are dark, and not light at all, outside of the spectrum. So again light and heat are supposed to depend on different kinds of molecular motions. So it may be with the nerve-cell activities. It may be that only those that are within certain limits of intensity, become sensations—causes of reflex action, or occasions of consciousness and perception. Or it may be that those that are sensations and those that are not, differ in kind, as heat, motion and light—motions in the molecules of bodies are supposed to differ from one another.

So with the nerve centres. There may be a great many forms and occasions of nerve-cell activity—which do not excite the mind to either consciousness or perception, or to any other mental act. There may be therefore many changes going on in the brain—a kind of "*cerebration*" of which we are unconscious, and of which we know nothing except what we infer from results.

Now, whether this kind of nerve-cell activity, in the hemispheres, will explain what Carpenter calls the phenomena of "unconscious cerebration," and others call "latent mental "action" or not, I will not attempt here to inquire. I proceed rather to one more thought which I wish to offer in concluding this Lecture.

That human beings are conscious of some of their mental acts and states is not denied. That there are many states of the nerve centres that excite to consciousness and other forms of mental activity, is not a matter of question. Nor do I think it any more a matter of question, that by far the largest part of these states or stages of activity do not occasion, and are not accompanied by consciousness. But is there consciousness in animals also? using the word in the sense in which we have been using it to denote a class of the phenomenon of human intelligence. I think not.

I do not propose to prove a negative. I propose rather to call attention to the state of the argument—the negative character of the argumentation—so to call it.

In human beings we assert consciousness on the ground of being conscious. I am not only conscious that I perceive, but I am conscious that I am conscious. Without consciousness there would be no intelligence—no affirmation—no assertion, and no denial even—of anything—no use of articulate language or intelligible signs *of thought.* Signs and proofs of *feeling* there of course, could be; for animal motion proves feeling in the lower sense of reflex emotion, at least. But it does not prove thought. Even if one could perceive without being conscious of it, he would not know that he perceived, and consequently would *know* neither himself nor the perceived object—he would perceive, but know nothing.

But in regard to dumb animals it is otherwise. *I* am conscious of mental action *within myself.* I am convinced that there is a like consciousness of mental action in other human beings—because they signify it to me, most unmistakably, by their language—articulate or otherwise. Not only have they a word for the class of mental acts which we call consciousness, but their language shows that they have experienced such phenomena. In fact I doubt whether there can be articulate language without consciousness. Parrot-like imitation of words there doubtless can be—but, I doubt if those processes of abstraction and generalization which occur in the origination of language, and in the intelligent acquisition of the use of it as well, ever occur or could occur without consciousness.

But animals have no such language. Their sounds and cries, as well as their acts, so far as we know, do not go beyond the expression of emotions, excito- and sensori-motor emotions. And acts of these two kinds may be performed in entire unconsciousness. We have spoken of the case of the motion of the foot on tickling it, in paralysis of the lower limbs. I suppose all persons have seen the spasmodic motions, and even heard the moaning sounds—which in some cases come to be articulate words, in the case of the sick and dying. These often occur when we can arouse the patient ; and then on inquiry we find that there was no consciousness of the motion or of the sound, no conscious intention to say anything, or call anybody's name.

Ferrier in his late work on "*The Functions of the Brain,*" has given the result of many exceedingly interesting experiments. He speaks of cases in which the brain down to the medulla oblongata was wholly removed, and yet the animal gave forth cries on pinching its toes, (pp. 26, 39, 67.) But the cries appeared to be purely mechanical, like those of an organ pipe, expressive of no emotion or feeling. He supposes they were produced by the reflex action that passes down the pneumogastric nerve to the diaphragm and inter-costal muscles. In some cases, as in cases of rabbits for instance, after the removal of the hemispheres, leaving the sensorium intact, sound was also produced ; but in this case it was a moaning piteous cry, as of sadness, rather than of sharp pain, (p. 68.) The sound was accompanied with feeling. But there was no consciousness. And Ferrier adds, (p. 247,) "I have repeatedly insisted "on the fact, that we are not to take mere reactions to sensory "impressions as indications of true sensation. If they are to "be so regarded, then we must clearly differentiate between "the lower animals and men. For it has been conclusively "demonstrated that in man, the consciousness of sensory im-"pressions, or true sensation, is a function of the cerebral "hemispheres."

I suppose that we must accept it as an established fact, that without the hemispheres there can be no consciousness, whether of sensations or of anything else. I accept the conclusion, though I cannot here give the proof in detail. Without the hemispheres there is no consciousness, and yet without them "animals," in the words of Ferrier, (p. 37,) "continue to per-"form actions differing little if at all from those manifested by "the same animals under absolutely normal conditions."

But it will be said that animals in their health, and in the perfection of their organism, act precisely as men do who are conscious of their activity. True indeed ; but then they act just as men do also, when they are *un*conscious and know nothing of their activity. Shall we then, go beyond the evidence and ascribe to mere dumb animals, a kind of mental activity, for the existence and reality of which we have no proof? The ascribing of consciousness to them is *our theory* for the explanation of their acts ; but it is only a theory. We are doubtless, led to it by appearances and the analogy of human actions. But in precisely the same way, mankind were led for thousands of years to ascribe a motion to the sun and the other heavenly bodies, which we now ***know*** they do not possess.

As already remarked, the discovery of the phenomena of the reflex action of the nervous centres, has done much already to revolutionize many of our most cherished psychological doctrines. I think it will go yet farther, and compel us to cease to ascribe consciousness to dumb animals at all—and to admit that in man also, there may be, and probably are, many changes in the nerve-cells of the brain, involving corresponding changes in the mental activity, of which we know nothing, when they occur—either by consciousness or otherwise.

It will doubtless be difficult for us to understand "animal "intelligence" in this view of it; difficult to comprehend how animals act as they do. But it is as difficult to comprehend what is below us, as what is above us, if they are both different in kind. It is as difficult, perhaps, to comprehend *animal* intelligence such as it is, as to comprehend the *divine* omniscience with its fore-knowledge and the freedom of moral actions. But I think we have the elements of both in ourselves. Omniscience is but the perfection of what is in us; and I fancy—I don't know—but I fancy that what we call animal intelligence is the same in kind as that which we ourselves experience in some of those moments of the most intense activity, when we do some things—sometimes even very extraordinary things—in a sort of waking somnambulism, with no consciousness of what we do at the time, and no recollection of it afterwards.

LECTURE III.

VOLITION.

Questions concerning the origin and nature of human action have occupied about as much attention, and occasioned about as much discussion and dispute as those that relate to the origin and foundations of human knowledge. And the question concerning the nature and prevalence of volition and voluntary action, properly so-called, seems to me to be one of those that are eminently demanding consideration, and some more definite agreement among psychologists and moralists, as well as in the speculations of physiologists and the mere students of Nature.

The discovery of the phenomena and laws of reflex action have introduced a new element into this discussion, if it has not given us facts that will totally revolutionize all our previous notions on the subject altogether.

We have seen that any recently produced condition of any of the tissues of the body, especially if it be painful, extends up to the gray matter of the spinal cord ; and is thence returned as an emotion or a motive tending to put the muscles concerned in the motion to which such a condition of the tissues should naturally give rise. This phenomena, we have seen, may occur in human life, when the patient is entirely unconscious of it, or of any part of it. It may occur also, in animals after the brain has been removed—after the spinal cord has been severed; and to some extent even after death; although in this case it requires, in all cases, I believe, the powerful stimulus of the electric current to produce the motion.

We have seen, also, that external objects, acting upon either of the five objective senses, touch, taste, smell, sight and hearing, may, *without producing any pain*, exert an influence upon the nerve centres in which the afferent nerves leading to the organs of those senses terminate—provided the afferent nerves of touch terminate (as I here claim that they do,) in the optic thalami—such as to cause the nerve-cells in those centres to send out a motive influence, or an emotion, which results in action, in the contraction of muscles, the movement of limbs, and even the utterance of cries. It is not quite so clear that this can take place, without either the spinal cord or the medulla oblongata. But there seems to be abundant proof that such phenomena can occur without the hemispheres; and with no consciousness of sensation, no perception, no mental act of any kind whatever. See Ferrier's "*Functions of the Brain,*" pp. 26, 39, etc.

There is, I think, a class of reflex actions in which the brain proper—the hemispheres—take part, called, as we have remarked in preceding Lectures, ideo-motor. I believe—though I am not so sure of it—that actions of this kind, can take place without our consent; and even against our will; and they occur also at times when we do all in our power to prevent them. The laughing at something ludicrous, when we are heartily ashamed of our apparent levity; the weeping when the grief seems unmanly, or the expression of it, a weakness that we would avoid at any cost, if we could, are examples of this kind of ideo-motor emotions. The nerve cells of the brain have been put into a state of activity which we neither desired, nor consciously produced, and which we would gladly have avoided, could we have done so.

Now, in *human* life, all action or motion, before birth, is of the first named kind, the lowest in the order, or excito-motor, and is occasioned by some effects produced in the tissues of the body, acting on the subjective sense—the sense of bodily condition. After birth, the objective senses, are, for a while, in such a condition that no external object makes any very definite impression upon them. But still they do make impressions; and we have almost immediately sensori-motor motions.

And soon, too,—but nobody can tell how soon—ideo-motor emotions ensue. And it is probable, nay, certain, that the brain exerts an influence upon the two other centres,—the spinal cord and the sensorium,—in the way of what is called "*inhibition*," if nothing else. But soon come the ideo-motor emotions; and as a result, emotions and actions that have their origin in the nerve-cell action of the hemispheres of the brain. And they are such as would never occur if there were no brain, or if there were not somewhere in the body nerve-cells that correspond to those which constitute the gray coating or cineritious matter of the hemispheres. I say in the brain, or somewhere else—for as Ferrier remarks, (p. 44,) in view of some reflex actions, which seem to be ideo-motor even when there are no hemisphere: "It is probable therefore, that in the ganglia of the invertebrates there are nerve cells which perform, "in however lowly a manner, the functions of the cerebral "hemispheres in the vertebrates."

And after a while too, there come both consciousness and volition. I am not sure which comes first, nor whether they do not come together. I think it doubtful if there is any consciousness, in the proper sense of the word, in the earliest days of human infancy. I doubt too, if there is any consciousness before there is volition, or any volition before consciousness. It is very likely that it is the exercise of volition that first awakes consciousness.

But with volition there comes a fourth kind of action ; or at least a fourth element that enters henceforward, into human experience, and largely into all human action. Seldom is any motor tendency, whether excito-motor, sensori-motor, or ideo-motor, so strong as to overcome the weight and inertia of a limb, and thus move it by the purely physical effect of the sensation transformed into reflex emotion alone ; and seldom is there any so strong that we cannot control them, and resist them, if we will.

This reflex action we know in ourselves—in two ways, or by two means. (1) We are conscious of it, and (2) we cognise the motions by the physical method, just as we do similar phenomena in lower animals. Even a paralyzed man can *see* his foot move as truly as he sees the frog jump, when the irritation used is applied to his hinder limb. But the voluntary element like consciousness itself, we know only by this faculty of interior observation, as it has been called, that is by consciousness, and by consciousness alone. Of course, therefore, in the exercise of this method or means of knowledge, each one of us, is observant of himself alone ; and he can apply the methods to no being, human or otherwise, besides himself. With regard to all others, the voluntary element is a matter of inference, and of inference only.

And as with consciousness so with volition also ; we *infer* volition in the case of our fellow men, from the language they use in describing what they know of their own actions. But in regard to the mere dumb animals, we are left to such inferences as we can draw from their actions alone. They often act as human beings do, and as human beings, voluntary agents might be supposed to do, if they were in the place of the animals. And this is all. It is much like the condition the human race were in before Copernicus. They supposed that the sun and stars rose and set; that was one way, *their* way, of accounting for the phenomena they observed. But objections were raised, arguments adduced, facts established, tending in the other direction, and now nobody believes the old theory.

With regard to human action, then, we have three causes—or classes of causes, the *one*, the tissues of our own bodies, their pains and aches, acting on the spinal cord and producing excito-motor emotions; and, of course, external objects may cause the pains and aches. *Second*, external objects acting through the objective senses, upon the sensorium and producing there sensations which those centres convert into sensori-motor emotions. We usually call the condition of the nerve centers in both these cases, a sensation. But these objects may extend their influence up to the hemispheres; and then not only do we become conscious of the sensations, and perceive the object that produced it; but there occurs also a state of the nerve-cell activity which we call *ideation* or an "idea" simply. This idea may also result in an ideo-motor emotion.

And then in the *third* place, we have the mind or the body as one of the forces that produce action. It acts on the nerve-cells of the hemispheres of the brain; and through them, on the afferent nerves that go to the muscles and glands of the body, producing in the one what we call *voluntary* action—or the voluntary element in human action—and in the other, those activities of the gland and the changes of the secretions which come from over exertion, preverse action, or the improper thoughts of the mind.

Now I think that in the three kinds of reflex action, namely, excito-motor, sensori-motor and ideo-motor, we have what writers in all ages have been accustomed to call INSTINCT.

Instinct has sometimes been regarded as opposed to, or contrasted with reason; and quite as often, perhaps, as contrasted with volition. It has seldom been defined; and no definition of it that has been given is generally accepted. The fact is, it has not been understood, and therefore it could not be defined. The word instinct has however been used to indicate, in a general and indistinct way, whatever any man or animal does naturally and not from any conscious reasoning or choice, concerning what he does do. But I think it will now be admitted that whatever we do in this way falls into one or the other of these three categories: excito-motor, sensori-motor or ideo-motor. And this is all the kinds or varieties of action that any one can recognise, who does not admit the existence of a mind which is self active and spontaneous in its nature.

There are, doubtless, activities in the nerve centres of different animals, as well as in those of human beings. And they consititute the peculiarities of their nature. For example, there is something in the sensorium or brain of a young duck whereby water is attractive, and induces the young bird to run and plunge into it, and enables it to swim at once, when in the water, without experience or instruction. But water repels the young of many other species of birds, so that they avoid it. All ruminants draw up the water they drink by suction. Cats and dogs lap theirs up with the tongue; and the one species, dogs, bend their tongues backwards, while the other, cats, bend theirs forward in the act of throwing the water into their mouths. No one can explain these differences, that I know of, but doubtless they are all instinctive, and all owing to some differences in the nerve centres of these animals.

And so of the thousand little, nameless traits and habits by which we never fail to discriminate one species of animals from another. They are doubtless, all of them, instinctive, determined by some peculiarity either of the nerve-cells or of their distribution and relations—and so fore-ordained in the very constitution and nature of the animals, each one by itself and "after its kind." This is shown by the two-fold fact (1) that when the young are taken from the mother before any possibility of education or imitation, they never fail to be like their parents in all the traits that characterize the species. (2.) The other fact is that by no amount of "variation under domestication," "natural selection," nor yet by climatic or other influences, so far as we know, can man or nature overcome or outdo those specific instincts and habits which are peculiar to the species and characteristic of it. Color and form may change; size may vary within almost any limiting extremes; new habits and instincts may be acquired or superinduced and transmitted through any number of generations. But after all, and through all, the peculiar traits and habits, motions, actions and instincts, that distinguish species from species, do not change, and apparently cannot be changed, except by the special act of the Creator Himself. Take for example two dogs, the most unlike of any that are called by that name, the largest and the smallest. let them differ never so much in form, in shape of head or limb, and in all the acquired habits as of hound and spaniel, setter and pointer, all that man has been able to educate them to, or to superinduce upon them, and it requires no anatomist to describe their osseous system, or to formulate their dentition, though differing as much as hippa-rion from a horse. We all know them to be dogs and nothing else, from their looks and their habits—their habits more than their looks—as soon as we see them. These things were predetermined in their very constitution, before man had control of them. And they remain in spite of all he can do, and so far as we know in spite of all the changes that "evolu-"tion" and "variation" can make. Mr. Darwin's most interesting and valuable books—have shown, as clearly as they have shown that there are wide variations under external ternal influences; that there are also certain specific traits and instincts—a fixity of character, hemming in each species by bonds and limits, beyond which there can be no variation.

And so I have no doubt it is with the differences in the mental capacities, preferences and tastes of mankind, whereby some are mathematicians and some are poets, by nature; some are naturalists and some linguists; some are artists, others are so awkward that they can do nothing as other people do it. These differences are all instinctive, pre-determined and fore-ordained in the very constitution of the nervous system of the individual—necessitated so far as he is concerned by some peculiarity of nerve cell, or nerve centre, over which he has but a limited control. Though he can restrain to some extent the manifestation of his peculiarities he cannot become wholly like another man.

But we must return to the consideration of the subject that is more immediately before us, Volition. Unless there were a mind in man—a something that is not inert like matter, but is spontaneous and self active, there could be neither consciousness nor volition. Knowledge, in any of its forms is not a function, a property, or a mode, of mere matter.

As soon as we become conscious at all we are conscious of volition and we know, if we reflect upon it at all, that we ourselves—this which I call I, or myself, is one of the forces that produce my action. I know, because I am conscious and have reflected upon it, that I think. I consider, reason for and against, and resolve or choose, that I will do something, and that as a consequence, my hands or my feet, my body or my tongue moves. And without that effort, they, in most of the ten thousand acts which I perform daily, would not move. I am conscious, in some cases of a reflex tendency to act in the same direction as my choice leads me. I am conscious in others of an effort to resist such tendency to action; and in some cases I become painfully conscious that, do the best I can, I cannot resist them—there will be involuntary—spasmodic actions—in spite of myself.

Now we may analyse these phenomena, as we please—we may contradict, deny or explain them away, as we please; but we cannot get rid of the fact that in them all, and in our very acts of analysis or contradiction, denial or explanation, there is a something that acts, that analyses, denies or affirms. And this something, we represent and denote by the pronoun I, when speaking of these acts as our own. This pronoun is in all dialects; it is an element in all languages; it represents an element—the agent—in all thought, and in all the personal actions of which we are conscious, and without it the thoughts and the actions could not be at all. It is a cause; we use the name of it as nominative to active verbs; *I* think, *I* speak, *I* walk, etc; and the consciousness of these acts of causation, it is probable, is what first gives us the thought of cause, and is moreover, what first suggested to us the idea of that spontaneity which, as a character of some acts and of some agents—a more extended analysis shows us must exist some where in the world where there is motion and change at all.

And this is more than reaction. When the experimenter pinched the frog's foot and the limb contracted it was a re-action of the spinal cord. When a strong light falls on the retina of the eye, the pupil will contract. This is a re-action of the nerve cells of the sensorium. And when the whole body leaps at a sudden fright, this too, is a re-action: in many cases it is only reaction, in which the cerebellum, if not the cerebum also, is concerned. But in volition there is more than re-action.

I do not know that we can choose without a motive. I presume we cannot. A pain in the foot reaches the spinal cord, and *moves* the foot, if the pain be intense enough. It may be so intense that we cannot if we try, hold the foot still. But it may not be intense enough to move the foot; it reaches the brain, *we* are conscious of the pain, *we* think the foot would be easier or less painful if it were lying in a different position; *we* put forth the effort, and move the foot. Our effort supplements the excito-motor emotion, and the foot moves—we have a motive for moving the foot.

Again, I see something coming towards my eye, the lid shuts; I can't help it. Perhaps the whole head moves. Perhaps also the effect which it produces, reaches the hemispheres of the brain, and, almost quicker than though, *I* move my head. I think it best to get it out of the way. The object in some way not only reaches the optic lobes, producing *sensation*, but the hemispheres also, producing *ideation*, as well.

It is certainly very possible that no act of volition takes place until some object, perceived, imagined, remembered or conceived, has excited the nerve-cells of the brain to a state of activity in which there is not only the mental acts of perception, imagination, conceptions, etc., but also some ideo-motor emotion or tendency to move the muscles. There is scarcely any object that can be perceived, or thought of, without some feeling, some emotion of some kind or another. This feeling is *a motive* to action ; and to the volition that precedes and produces the action. It is also in its physical aspect, an ideo-motor emotion.

But in very few if in any of these cases is the re-action—the reflex tendency to action of which the object itself may properly be said to be the cause, and the occasion merely, sufficient to move the limb, carrying the weight and inertia of the part of our body which is concerned in the motion. And we are conscious of supplying the rest of the force that is rendered. *We* move the hand or the foot. *We* set the tongue in motion, and guide it in the articulation of the words we utter.

I am well aware of the fact that we must make a distinction between the consciousness of a mental act or state, and our judgment concerning its character. We often call our mental acts and states by names which indicate almost anything but their real character. Men call mere acts of fancy, insight or intuition. They speak of having an idea, and of being conscious of it too, when they really *have* nothing, but are only *thinking* of something. A man may easily mistake anger which is purely a personal feeling, for indignation which is of a much higher character. So too, we often meet with cases in which we cannot help thinking that one mistakes and miscalls his pride and self-conceit by the name of humility. But I do not see how one can be mistaken in supposing that he makes an effort when he does not make any. The act is simple, as simple as sensation, perception, or as consciousness itself. It can hardly be mistaken for re-action—for we are perhaps the most conscious of effort, when we are making the greatest effort to resist and control the re-actions which external objects would occasion by the sensations and ideas they produce in us.

Effort is moreover a simple act. It makes one of the three cöordinate classes of the phenomena of which we are conscious, sensation or feeling, perception or thought, and volition or effort. The three are unlike in kind. Neither of them can be resolved into the other. Neither of them can be mistaken for the other ; and, as I believe, it results from the law or condition of cöordination in cognition, that neither one of them could have been thought of by any human being, or would have had a name in any human language, if only the other two had been matter of experience.

We may reach the same conclusion with regard to this psychological fact in another way.

I have spoken of reflex action as the result of a re-action of tha great nerve centres, It is not, however, as I have explained elsewhere, so much in the nature of a mechanical *re-action* as in the nature of a physical conversion of one force into another. A ball thrown against the wall is repelled instantly ; the re-action is instantaneous, and equal to the action. But in the physico-chemical sciences, re-action or transformation is not always instantaneous. A feeble current of electricity will, in time, charge a very large Leyden jar. A piece of platinum into which a current of electricity is passing, grows warm gradually, especially if the platinum bar is large and the current is small. But it gradually heats up to the point where radiation becomes equal to the rate of increase of heat occasioned by the continuance of the electric current.

So it seems to be with the nerve centres. The intensity of the sensation increases in some cases, with the continual activity of a cause until it reaches its highest point of intensity; and that point in many cases, becomes so high that we cannot control our actions; they become involuntary and spasmodic —we act whether we will or not, and we cannot help acting in accordance with the reflex impulse.

But we can easily suppose a case in which there is no such increase of intensity, and yet there is a result which shows an increase of effort. In fact, it is obvious, that all through life, we do not put forth effort in proportion to the value of that which we seek—but rather in proportion to our estimate of the difficulty to be overcome, in the way of getting it. However valuable or necessary an object may be, we put forth but little effort when we know that it can be obtained with perfect certainty and with ease. But let us take a simple case. Suppose there is something on the floor that offends me, my eyes or my nose, and I stoop down with the purpose of picking it up and tossing it out of the window. I suppose it to be loose on the floor and weighing but a few grains. I put forth effort accordingly—but it does not come. I put forth more effort until I exert strength enough to raise the object, or find that it is too heavy for me to raise it at all. Now here was an increase of effort, *with a change of thought*, but there was no corresponding change in the *motive*. The object did not become more offensive meanwhile. Nor was there time enough for the sensation to intensify up from a strength sufficient to raise a few grains, to that which is required to raise as many pounds. With *no* change therefore, in the force of the motive, or one that is inconsiderably small, there was a great change in the effort I made. Hence, the I, that made the effort must be a real and an efficient cause. And not only so, it must be a spontaneously-acting cause; there was nothing but thought and volition in the case, that varied or changed. *I* thought to do it, and *I* willed to do it, and *I* did it. The offensive object did not move itself out of my way; nor did it move me to move it, as steam and water move the machinery that accomplishes the wonders of modern manufacture. There was a force within, supplementing the force without, cöoperating with it, in this case, although it might have acted in the opposite direction.

All mere matter is *now* considered as acting under the law of inertia. If a mass or a molecule is at rest, no physicist expects that it will change from a state of rest to a state of motion without the action of some force from without itself. If two substances, as oxygen and hydrogen are mixed and in contact, and yet not acting upon each other, no chemist supposes they will begin to act until something external to them acts upon them and changes their condition, by pressure, by heat, by light, by electricity, or by something of the kind.

But this law cannot hold throughout the universe. It may pertain to all mere matter; and in fact it is the doctrine of modern science that it does so extend, and mark off the limits of mere matter and the material phenomena of change and motion. But there must be somewhere something that does not act under this law, or rather, perhaps we should say something that is not confined to, and limited by this law. Professor Pierce, of Harvard, in his great work on "*Analytic Mechanics*," begins his treatise with these words: "Motion is "an essential element of all physical phenomena; and its "introduction into the universe of matter was necessarily the "preliminary act of creation, the earth must have remained "forever without form and void; and eternal darkness must "have been upon the face of the deep, if the spirit of God "had not first *moved* upon the face of the waters." And he closes his Book with these words: "But it is time to return to "nature and learn from her actual solutions, the recondite "analysis of the more obscure problems of celestial and phys- "ical mechanics. In these researches there is one lesson "which cannot escape the profound observer. Every portion "of the material universe is prevaded by the same laws of me- "chanical action, which are incorporated into the very consti- "tution of the human mind, the solution of the problem of "this universal presence of such a spiritual element is obvious "and necessary. THERE IS ONE GOD, AND SCIENCE IS THE "KNOWLEDGE OF HIM."

From this it would appear as though the study of the phenomena and laws of motion and change in nature would lead to, and suggest, the conception of a spontaneous cause—of a something that is not material, and does not act under the purely physical law of action and reaction, as being equal and in opposite directions—a something that can begin to act when not acted upon, and can increase the intensity of its action, and the strength of its effort, *at will*, and with the mere knowledge that such an increase is demanded by the emergency of the occasion. The nature of the Personal Cause may be suggested in this way, it would seem, as well as by the consciousness of spontaneous activity within ourselves. But doubtless we could have no very adequate conception of it without the experience of its exercise which we get from the consciousness of that spontaneous activity which takes place within us nearly every moment of our waking lives.

I have expressed the opinion that consciousness is an *im*mediate source or means of knowledge, and that it is in reality the only immediate source. Philosophers have disagreed and disputed much, as to what is *im*mediate knowledge—what are the objects of it. But they have never disagreed that I know of, as to the fact that such knowledge, whatever it may be, neither requires proof, nor admits of denial. Whether it be the "inate ideas" of the schoolmen and Descartes, the "idea-"images" of Locke, or the "sensations" of Condillac and Hume—our knowledge of them is admitted to be absolute. It admits of no proof—because nothing can be better known as a means whereby to prove it. And it admits of no denial—because the effort at denial would put one in the awkward condition either of being unconsciously conscious or consciously unconscious.

Sense-perception at any rate, is certainly *mediate* and depends on sensation. It may be modified by any change in the organs of sense. It depends largely on a process of reasoning also. Hence we can have no *im*mediate knowledge of the objects in the external world. Nor, of course, can any knowledge be called *immediate* which depends upon reasoning and inference. This would seem to reduce all *im*mediate knowledge to the two classes, (1) the acts and states of our own minds of which we are conscious, and (2) those intuitive *a priori* judgments which constitute the self-evident axioms and first principles of all branches of knowledge. Besides these two I know of no other. I do not see how there can be any other.

But we cannot if we would deny a fact of consciousness. The effort would be like that of the man who after having been knocked over, vociferously proclaimed himself, "*not dead, but "speechless.*" We may vary our explanation of these facts, give them different names, and refer them to one or another class; but we cannot deny their existence. The fact of volition or conscious self-activity, we cannot deny or explain, in any way that will enable us to get rid of the characteristic I am ascribing to it. Say what you will you cannot avoid saying *I*, *I* did it, or *I* did not do it, *I* affirm, or *I* deny. *I* doubt, or *I* believe. In all ways and under all forms of expression the I, the *ego,* the conscious self—or the self-conscious person, appears, standing prominently out or necessarily implied in the very substratum and indispensable condition of our assumption. When we can banish all personal pronouns from any human language, or speak of what we do without using the pronoun I, or its equivalent, we may claim to really disbelieve in volition ; but not as I think, before.

But we have not the same grounds or reasons for ascribing volition or voluntary action to dumb animals. If they have volition and are conscious of it, they have not the means of making it known to us. *They use no personal pronouns.* I am conscious of volition in myself, and as a part of my own experience. The language that my fellow men use, makes me equally sure of such an element in their experience. But when we come to dumb animals it is only an inference from their actions. It is only *our* theory for explaining them.

So long as the nature of reflex action was unknown, there was, perhaps, no way explaining what appears to be animal intelligence and voluntary action, but by ascribing those phenomena as seen in animals, to the same psychological conditions as in man. The question of "instinct and reason" was discussed, much discussed, but nowhere was there a clear line of distinction drawn between them. It was a matter of dispute whether they differed in kind, or only in degree. It was supposed and held that men have some instincts, and it was thought to be equally certain that animals have some reason or intelligence.

But the discovery of the machinery of reflex action in the animal frame, and the laws and nature of that action, has put the whole subject of animal intelligence and animal action in a new light. It has shown us an entirely new set of phenomena, which we cannot neglect to take note of. It has shown that, however we may continue to call it, all of animal instinct except perhaps a part of the very highest, may be mere reflex action, and may imply neither mind, nor thought, nor intelligence, nor will; and that so far at least, the actions of animals need not be regarded or called either rational or voluntary.

And the question arises how far may this explanation go in accounting for the higher forms of action? I agree entirely with Professor Huxley in his article in *The Popular Science Monthly* already quoted, as far as his conclusions apply to dumb animals. And he teaches that animals are only *automata;* that is, mere machines—without intelligence or volition, as we have been using these terms. If there is no mind, as a substantial thing, different in kind from the body, there can be no volition, no voluntary action, no spontaneity, nothing but reflex action, which is merely re-action to the sensible objects around them, and to the condition of the tissues of their own bodies. And most assuredly all the tendencies of experiments and observations in regard to reflex action and the functions of the nerve centres are in the direction of Huxley's conclusion, so far as mere dumb animals are concerned.

I have made no original investigations or explorations in this department myself. But I have eagerly sought and carefully studied the accounts given of the researches of others and their inferences from them; and I believe that they confirm this general statement, that the effect of removing the hemispheres is *merely* to render the animal more stupid. It does not deprive the animal of any one class of functions or actions, which it was capable of performing before. In the case of the frog, spoken of by Huxley, he says, "It will starve sooner "than feed itself, although if food is put into its mouth, it "swallows it." Dalton says, "the effect of this mutilation is "simply to plunge the animal into a profound stupor, in which "he is almost entirely inattentive to surrounding objects ; the "bird (he is speaking of a pigeon,) remains motionless upon "his perch, or standing on the ground with its eyes closed, "and the head sunk between the shoulders." (*Physiology*, p. 405.) Ferrier, one of the latest authorities on the subject—the latest in fact that I have seen—says, (p. 34, 35,) of a frog—from which the hemispheres had been removed, "Deprived of its "cerebral hemispheres, the frog will maintain its normal atti- "tude, and resist all attempts to displace its equilibrium. If "laid on its back it will immediately turn on its face and re- "gain its station on its feet. If placed on a board and the "board be tilted in any direction, the animal will make the "appropriate bodily movements, to throw its centre of gravity "within the basis of support. If the foot be pinched, it will "leap away. If it be thrown into the water it will swim until "it reaches the side of the vessel, and then clambers up and "sits perfectly quiet. If its back be stroked gently it will ut- "ter loud croaks, and this with such uniformity on each appli- "cation of the stimulus, that as Goltz indicates, a chorus of "brainless frogs might be obtained, which would utter their "[chorus] on the appropriate occasion in a manner that would "have delighted the heart of Aristophanes." . . "If placed "at the bottom of a pail of water, it will ascend to the surface "to breathe. And not merely so, but if placed in a vessel "inverted over a pneumatic trough, containing a column of "water sustained by barometric pressure, it will ascend to the "surface as before; but not finding there the necessary atmos-"pheric air, it will work its way downwards and succeed in "making its escape out of the vessel to the free surface of the "trough. There is a method in its movements. If an obsta-"cle be placed between it and the light of a window, the frog "will not spring blindly against the obstacle, when its toe is "pinched, but will clear it and spring to the side. It will al-"ter the course of its leap according to the position of the "obstacle between it and the light. *There is so far no differ-"ence between its behaviour and that of a frog in the full posses-"sion of all its faculties.* But yet a very remarkable difference "is perceptible; the brainless frog, unless disturbed by some "peripherical stimulus, will sit forever quiet in the same spot, "and become converted into a mummy. *All spontaneous ac-"tion is annihilated.* Its past experience has been blotted out, "and it exhibits no fear in circumstances which otherwise "would cause it to retire or flee from danger. It will sit quite "still if the hand be put forth cautiously to seize it; but it "will retreat if a brusque movement is made close to its eyes." The italics are my own.

I have given above from Dalton, an account of the appearance of a pigeon from which the hemispheres had been removed. Ferrier, p. 38, gives a very similar account. But on p. 35, he speaks thus of a fish: "A fish so mutilated main-"tains its normal equilibrium in the water, and uses its tail "and fins in swimming, with as great percision and co-ordina-"tion as before. The brainless fish is, however, continually on "the move, and there is also method in its movements. It "will not run its head against any obstacle placed in its path, "but turn to the right or left according to circumstances.

"Left to itself in the water, it swims in a straight line, and, "unlike other fishes which loiter by the way, smelling of this, "and nibbling at that, it keeps on its course, as if impelled by "some irresistible impulse, and only stops when it reaches the "side of the vessel, or when worn out by pure nervousness and "fatigue." Ferrier also adds some few items to those given by Dalton, in his account of the pigeon. After speaking of the profound sleep, he says, (p. 36), "From this state of repose "it is easily awakened by a gentle push or pinch, and looks "up and opens its eyes. Occasionally, apparently without "any external stimulation it will look up and yawn. . . . "Should a fly happen to settle on its head it will stroke it off," etc. And on p. 37, he repeats the assertion [the animals] "continue to perform actions in many respects differing little, "if at all, from those manifested by the same animals under "absolutely normal conditions."

As, however, we ascend in the scale, the difference between the two conditions of the animals becomes greater. And yet in no case that he describes or alludes to, does he show anything that militates against the general statement I have made above, namely, the only observed or known difference is one of degree only, and not one of kind; the animal becomes more stupid and inefficient—but it does not lose any one entire class of mental or psychological phenomena. It must be remembered, however, that Ferrier has included "dogs," which are regarded as among the highest in the scale of animal intelligence, in the remarks I have quoted in regard to the effects of a total removal of the hemispheres. They become only a *little more stupid*, a *little more incapable* of co-ordinate action, "though the fact of emotional response to sensory impressions "points," as he remarks, "to the conclusion that we have to "deal not with the complete absence, but only with a suspen- "sion of the other forms of functional activity," p. 40.

These phenomena have led to the conjecture that consciousness and volition may exist in other centres besides the hemispheres. But the suggestion meets no favor, and is in fact entirely disproved. Ferrier says, p. 45, "we obviously cannot "obtain any answer to the queston—whether the hemispheres "are necessary for sensation and consciousness—when the "functions of the hemispheres are so affected as to prevent the "expression in words or by gestures, language of subjective "states, if any such really exist. But we have experiments of "disease [in man] which practically detach the hemispheres "from the mesencephalic connections, and leave thought and "speech intact, so that we can obtain direct testimony in re- "gard to the consciousness of impressions. . . When this "occurs, the individual has absolutely no consciousness of "tactile impressions, . . *however much he may strain his at- "tention to receive them*." And he says elsewhere, (p. 248,) "It has been conclusively demonstrated that, *in man*, the con- "sciousness of sensory impression . . is a function of the "cerebral hemispheres." The italics are my own.

And the statement is reiterated in various forms, p. 40. "When the hemispheres are removed, all the actions of the "animal become the immediate and necessary response to the "form and intensity communicated to its afferent nerves." p. 121. "Removal of the cerebral hemispheres . . reduces "the animal to the condition of a machine."

There seems to be no doubt, therefore, that all, or nearly all the acts that an animal ever performs, may be performed after that which has been demonstrated to be the only organ and centre of consciousness and volition has been removed. The only question that remains, I believe, is in regard to the instinct of reproduction. As yet no proof has been discovered of its retention. But this is not important, it seems to me. The state of stupidity and inaction which always ensues upon the operation, is, I think, a sufficient explanation of the non-appearance of any manifestations of that kind.

But what I chiefly note is the fact that there is not the loss of any *one class* of acts or instincts ; but only a stupefaction of them all, and of one about as much as another. If a man loses his eyes he becomes blind—one entire class of his psychological experiences is gone. It is not a general stupefaction ; but is the loss of one class or kind of forms of activity —with perhaps, a quickening of the rest. With the loss of the hemispheres in animals it is otherwise. No entire species or kind of experiences is gone—they all remain, only they are impaired in intensity.

With man, however, it is otherwise. With the inactivity of the brain, as in the case of tumor, abscess, congestion, or any cause producing coma, there is a total loss of consciousness, of volition, and of all that one knows by consciousness, and by that exclusively, to be a part of his experience. The spinal cord remains active; the sensorium re-acts, and the patient is like an animal with the brain removed ; only the change is greater, the stupidity more profound, the inaction more complete, as we should naturally expect would be the case, from the greater size of the brain in proportion to the other parts of the nervous system. But all intelligence proper, all consciousness at the time, all recollection afterwards, and all volition are at an end. Excito-motor and sensori-motor action remain—but probably there is no reaction of the hemispheres—or ideo-motor action in such cases at all. The contrast between men and animals is complete and entire, the one only becomes more sluggish and stupid—the other loses one entire class of vital phenomena—and that one the most characteristic of all—the facts and phenomena of consciousness.

I think then, we must admit that we have no authority for ascribing volition and voluntary action to animals, in any of the ordinary functions of their lives. They are all instinctive, all mere reflex actions, mere manifestations of physical phenomena.

And this leads me to question whether ideo-motor action, as defined by Carpenter, in the passage cited in a former Lecture, (p. 32,) is really found in animals in their ordinary instincts and actions at all. The Brain is undoubtedly, a reservoir of power, a sort of Leyden jar of nerve activity, for animals as for men. But I doubt if there is ordinarily any purely ideo-motor reaction from that centre, in animals below man.

It will be noted that Carpenter speaks of it as manifested in man. He says, "objects which give rise to *our* sensations," "*we* begin to form ideas," etc, and "these ideas may express "themselves in action, as we see in the case of the somnambu- "list, etc. It is true Carpenter ascribes it to animals, such as are, in his words, "governed by intelligence." But it seems to me to be a fact, inferred from the discoveries made since he wrote, that there is nothing in that "*intelligence*" that differs in kind from what the same animals perform, after the hemispheres have been entirely removed or have become paralyzed by disease, so as to preclude the possibility of any ideo-motor actions as defined by Carpenter.

These views are confirmed by the experiments of Ferrier. He claims to have found three regions of the hemispheres, an antero-frontal, as he calls it, an occipital, and a middle region.

From the middle or central region he gets, by stimulation of the cortical covering of gray matter, responses in the way of reflex action. But from the antero-frontal—the forehead part, which is the seat and organ of intelligence in man, he gets no response whatever in the form of reflex action. It is of this part of the brain he is speaking, when he says, p. 231, "Removal or destruction of the antero-frontal lobes is not followed by any definite physiological results. The animals retain their appetites and instincts, and are capable of exhibiting emotional feeling. . . The powers of voluntary motion (in his sense of voluntary,) are retained in their integrity." . . The animals were selected on account of their "intelligent character. After the operation, though, they "might seem to one who had not compared their present with "their past, fairly up to the average of monkey intelligence, "they had undergone a considerable psychological alteration." This change, however, consisted, as I have already stated, chiefly in their disposition "to remain in an apathetic, dull condition," "dozing off to sleep," "a form of mental degradation which "may be reduced in ultimate analysis to loss of the faculty of "attention," p. 288.

But the question remains with regard to those more remarkable instances, which are always cited and referred to in such discussions, as proof of intelligence and volition. The case which Carpenter cites, of his horse, which learned to take the pump handle in his mouth and raise water for himself and others to drink, is a good one. The case of a cat, I once had, in another. The wire from the door knob passed along the banisters of the stairs, that led from the hall to the basement. The bell was in sight; the cat learned to stand on the stairs, and with one fore paw on the banister, he would catch the other hold of the wire and ring the bell, whenever he wanted to have the door opened so that he might get into the parlor.

These cases seem like reasoning, and are commonly cited as proof it. If there were volition in the cases, there will be no doubt, I presume, that there was intelligence and reasoning as well. In fact, I doubt whether there can be volition at all, without intelligence and reasoning. And no one, so far as I know, would ascribe voluntary action to an animal without at the same time ascribing to it reasoning and intelligence also.

Well, why not? This is the natural question.

As preliminary to any answer, we must consider the fact that acts which are clearly reflex, and only reflex, differ so little from those that are voluntary, that there is no possibility of distinguishing the one from the other, by the purely *physical* method. I presume there is no reflex action, that may not be successfully imitated, voluntarily. I know of none—and I know of no " voluntary action " so called, that may not be produced under circumstances which entirely and absolutely preclude the supposition that there is any volition or conscious thought in its production. I have cited Huxley's striking article in a preceding Lecture, and I have cited statements somewhat like his from Ferrier in this. Huxley, it is true, had, or is supposed to have had, a motive in advocating his views. Animals without the hemispheres can perform acts which *appear* to indicate intelligence and volition—they perform them, as he says, " with great care and deliberation." And then, on the next page but one, he speaks of a man acting under circumstances where intelligence and volition are precluded, and he says, " I show you a case of a man performing actions evi- " dently more complicated and mostly more *rational* (the ital- " ics are my own) than any of the ordinary operations of ani-

"mals; and yet you have positive proof that these actions are "merely mechanical." If then, animals and men, without consciousness and volition, can perform such acts, all acts in fact, that are ordinarily supposed to imply volition and thought, we can have no good reason for ascribing volition and thought to any body. And if there is no reason for ascribing thought and volition—there can be no reason, *a fortiori*, for ascribing a mind which can reason and choose. Well, if we are limited to the physiological method, or if we intentionally and purposely (I will not say preversely) confine ourselves to that method, Huxley is right, and there can be no successful refutation of his conclusion.

The "naturalist" with one eye on his microscope, and the other shut that he may see the better, *sees* brains and can see only brains. He sees that even the lowest vertebrate has the rudiment at least of a brain. Fishes have one that is quite distinctly developed. Birds and reptiles have a larger one; and in mammals the brain becomes marked by convolutions and its hemispheres are connected by a somewhat massive commissure. And in man it only reaches a larger size and a higher development. If then, brain is the organ of mind, we find mind, with its inseparable elements—intelligence, consciousness and volition, in all the orders of the vertebrates. And even below them, there are nerve-cells "which perform, in "however lowly a manner, the functions of the cerebral hemispheres." (Ferrier, p. 44.)

But would it not be better for the naturalist to open the other eye and look within himself; and *see* there, facts of another order and of an entirely different significance? We see there facts in ourselves, which, however, it may be elsewhere, disclose to us a something that does think and choose. We find proof of volition or rather not proof of volition—but volition itself. By this method we know volition, more certainly, than we can possibly know, by the other method, any of the facts that are supposed to prove volition. In this method there is but one step—we are *immediately*] conscious of the volition. In the other there are two, (1) conscious of the perception, and (2) the act of precepticn itself, with our inferences from it. In the first method there can be no error. In the last there is always the possibility of false perception and mistaken inference.

But it is time to proceed to consider some of the reasons for denying intelligence and volition to animals, over and above the mere fact that we can account for all of their actions as reflex, and without volition.

In the first place the animals that perform such unusual acts do not show any more intelligence in respect to other things than those that exhibit no such feats. With the human child, when it attains the intelligence to do any one thing, it at once shows the intelligence, by doing other things of a like grade. There is a gradual growth and development of intelligence. But this is not at all the case with these animals. I have no doubt they are generally among the most "intelligent" of their species—above the average. But they develope no general intelligence—no superior skill or instincts in regard to other things that require intelligence, and are just as necessary for their welfare and their comfort, as the one that is spoken of as so remarkable.

In the next place, I can see no reason why, if these animals possess so much intelligence as is thus ascribed to them, they should not have a language. Certainly these mental processes, which they are supposed to possess, imply enough, in the way of analysis, abstraction and generalization—all of which are implied in any act of reasoning—to give rise to a set of sounds or signs "to express their ideas" with—or if not enough to enable them to invent one, enough at least to learn and adopt one from man.

And finally, I think there can be no doubt, that if they possessed so much intelligence as this theory of their acts implies, they would come to have an education that would result in the acquisition of knowledge, that might be transmitted from generation to generation, as is the case with man. It is not a question now, whether there is not an improvement in their physical constitution from generation to generation—resulting in an improvement of instincts, as I have explained the word. Such an improvement undoubtedly, has occurred in many of the kinds of domesticated animals, and may not unlikely have occurred in the wild animals also. But such improvement is not at all like in kind, that which the human family have made in the discoveries of science, or which they perpetuate by the education of their children, in what they themselves have learned.

I think, therefore, that these extraordinary cases constitute no exception to the rule that all such acts are merely instinctive, and that instinct is reflex action, and that only. It is not unlikely that in these cases the hemispheres may re-act, or respond to sensations in a way that becomes common and perfectly normal in man—though rare and exceptional in the animals below him. The brain re-acts in these cases in a way in which man can and does voluntarily cause it to *act* whenever, in the exercise of his judgment, he comes to think it best, and to choose so to act. I think, therefore, that neither consciousness nor volition, nor voluntary action in the proper scientific sense of these words can be ascribed to any animal below man, and that all language that seems to ascribe to them voluntary action—or to speak of voluntary action as belonging to animals, is the result of a misinterpretation of the facts that are observed. And it requires no words to show how extensive a change in our theories and discussions would be required by the adoption of this view of volition and voluntary action.

Of course, we cannot expect any change in the current language of the people on this subject. It was at best, a hundred years after Copernicus had promulgated the true theory of the apparent changes in the heavenly bodies, before it was fully adopted, even by *scientific* men. Bacon, who lived nearly a century later than Copernicus, did not accept the theory, [C., born in 1473, and B. in 1561.] And even now we continue to speak of the sun and moon and stars, as *rising* and *setting*, etc., as though the motion which causes these apparent changes were theirs, and not our own. But I think that for scientific purposes, we must cease to speak of voluntary action in animals, and cease to ascribe to them volition in any sense of the word, until we have some other and better proof of its existence than we now have, or can ever expect to have, without other means of observation or proof than seems likely ever to become possible for us. We *know* that in man there is consciousness, reasoning and volition—in animals we have no proof of these elements, and reasons, which, are, at least, *very strong*, for denying their existence.

LECTURE IV.

INSIGHT.

I propose to devote the remaining Lectures of this Course, to a brief consideration of the three great questions in Metaphysics, that remain as yet unsettled. I intend to offer a solution and answer to them—differing in some respects from any that have ever yet been proposed—which as I believe after much and prolonged consideration, will in the end be accepted and prove satisfactory. These answers, as I think, will not only settle these questions for metaphysical purposes—but they will also, I hope, supply a new basis for some very important physical inductions and theories, and lead to results differing in some respects from the doctrines now held.

The questions, as previously stated, relate to, 1. The nature and origin of knowledge. 2. The ground and extent of certainty, or absolute truth. 3. The nature and limits of real causes.

I propose to devote a Lecture to each of these subjects respectively.

I think we may assume that all knowledge is, or may be expressed in language. This may not be true of feeling or of mere sentiment. It may not be true of the products of imagination or of fancy. But I think it is true, beyond question or peradventure, of whatever comes within the domain of knowledge.

Language consists of words; and words, for our purpose,

may be divided into two classes—names—which denote the objects or things we speak about, and the other, includes whatever other parts of speech there are in use, or may be needed, in order to construct and articulate the names into sentences, so that what we say of things will represent them as they appear to us, or as we think and believe them to be, in themselves and in their relations to each other.

For the present I shall consider the names only. And this I do the more readily, because in the controversy with regard to the origin of knowledge, names have been selected and put forward, on the one side, and accepted on the other, as tests, as I have remarked in a previous Lecture, and shall have occasion to consider again, before I get through with the subject.

Names then, are considered as denoting things. And I shall assume for the present, that all objects of immediate knowledge are denoted by names; that is, whatever we know immediately, is denoted by a name.

But of these objects we always predicate adjectives, as snow is white, the table is hard, the orange is round, etc. And, in fact, we cannot cognize any object without *so* cognizing it that we can, by acts of analysis and judgment, which I need not now explain, predicate and affirm of it some property. In short, we cannot know *that* anything is—without knowing, to some extent, at least, *what* it is.

Hence, while names denote the things that we cognize or know, the adjectives that we may predicate of them, denote what we know of them.

The same is undoubtedly true of verbs to some extent. But then, verbs can always be expressed, or at least replaced, by adjectives, without harm or loss, so far as our present purpose is concerned. Thus, if I say, John walks, I can also say, John is walking.

Now, all the adjectives, (including the verbs if we choose,) that we use, or all those at least, that we can use to express what we know of things, may be resolved or divided into four classes—with reference to their origin, and their relation to the subject before us.

1st. We have what we may call the *objective* adjectives, such as denote the sensible properties, the properties by which objects appear to us, and are cognized and perceived in sense-perception, as hard, soft, round, square, hot, cold, wet, dry, etc., including in this class every sensible property, every one, which, in accordance with the common use of language, we can be said to know by the senses.

2d. We have what may be called the *subjective* adjectives—such as indicate our feelings towards an object; as beautiful, frightful, etc. These adjectives, neither give, nor express, any knowledge concerning the objects of which they are predicated. They indicate only *our feelings* towards the objects. And as the origin of the objective adjectives is accounted for by reference to sensation and perception, so these are to be accounted for by reference to the sensibility or emotional part of our nature.

3d. There is a class of adjectives that denote the relations of one thing to another, as heavy, hard, near, distant. These we may call *relative* adjectives. In this class I include all those adjectives and verbs, that are used to denote that knowledge of things which we get from our observation of their relations to, and actions upon one another. In this class, therefore, will be included most, if not all, those terms that are used to denote the physical and the chemical properties of bodies. And there may be occasion to subdivide them into two classes, as (a) such as relate to place and time, as far, near, early, late, etc., and (b) such as denote *active* properties, including all those that are learned by an observation of the actions of objects upon one another.

4th. And finally, there is a class that denote properties and relations that can be derived from no one of the sources named above—namely, mere sense-perception of the objects, as the *objective* properties, mere feeling, occasioned by the objects, as the *subjective* properties, nor yet the mere observation of their effects on one another, or on our own bodies, as is the case with the *active* properties. Those properties I propose to call—for the want of a better name—*metaphysical* properties.

Now, if we had only the first three classes of adjectives, I presume no question would ever have arisen, as to the origin of ideas. All words in use, could easily have been traced to and accounted for by reference to "sensation and reflection," (and to sensation alone, for all sense-perception is based upon and conditioned by sensation,) by one or the other of the three different mental process, that follow upon sense-perception, (1) analysis and abstraction, (2) æsthesis or feeling, (3) comparison of objects one with another. Thus far we have no word and no element of knowledge that cannot be traced to "sensation and reflection" as explained by Locke, and fully accounted for by his theory.

It is, however, a question which I will not discuss here, whether with only sensation and reflection—taking the word "reflection," in Locke's sense, there could be any of the mental processes just spoken of. I think there could not. But I prefer to waive that question, for the present; as its discussion is not important to the undertaking now before us.

Let us take for our first example the word "*shortest*" as used in the proposition—"the straight line is the shortest between two points."

I am aware that "*shortestness*" can hardly be called a metaphysical property. The word is derived etymologically, from the adjective short, which may be regarded as denoting a relative or comparative, property. But this word suits my present purpose better than any other one that has occurred to me, and better, in some respects, perhaps, than if it denoted a metaphysical property.

No one, I presume, will doubt the proposition just cited "a straight line is the shortest line that there can be between any two points." But how do we know this? Suppose that we admit that "straightness" is an objective, or—which is the same thing a word that denotes—a sensible property—so that we can, not only see the line, but also see that it is straight. We may also see that it is "short" so that the adjective "short" may denote only a relative property. But how about "short-"estness"? This cannot be seen by the eye. It cannot be ascertained by measurement or comparison; for all our means of measurement and comparison fall short of that absolute exactness and certainty which we not only obtain, but unhesitatingly and inexorably demand, in mathematics.

How then do we know that the straight line is the shortest? I think we are now face to face, with the phenomena we are in quest of. We certainly know the fact—we can demonstrate it, if any body doubts, disputes or questions it. And yet we cannot make it perceptible to the senses; or measure it to a difference, which, in the language of the mathematicians is "less "than any assignable quantity." It is a proposition which "experience," if we limit the word, as Locke, Mill, and the men of that school necessarily do and must, has not taught us, and never can teach us. The reasons just given prove this. If we cannot either see or measure to an exactness that is nearer than any assignable difference, and which—whatever mathematicians may find it convenient to regard it, is yet ontologically something. There must be some means of knowledge, besides sense-perception, and any reasoning we can base upon it.

I think we shall see, if we look at the facts,—that we do somehow, see, know, and affirm, the truth of the proposition, just as soon as we understand the import of its terms. Nor is this all. We affirm it with a confidence in its certainty, that we do not feel in any proposition that affirms a merely sensible property. We all know and admit that "the senses may deceive "us;" that we may be mistaken, possibly, in regard to what we see or hear, even when we feel the most confident. There is a false-perception, to which we are all liable. But in this case we feel that there is no mistake, no chance for false perception, no dependence upon conditions, times and places; but always, everywhere, and under all circumstances, the straight line is the shortest. We feel and declare that this is an absolute truth.

But *how* do we know it? This is the real question. I do not think that any theory of "*innate ideas*" of "*schemata*" or of *a priori* "conceptions" will much help us. Suppose we admit that any one of them, or all of them are real—what good can they do us? How do we know that they are what they claim to be? How do we know that they are true and trustworthy? No answer has been given; and no answer as I think, can be given, that does not assume something that needs proof quite as much as the theory that is to be proved by it.

My answer is as follows: there is an act of insight—not mere *intuition*, for that is a looking *upon* a thing—but an act of *insight* or seeing *into* things, that goes along with the act of perception or imagination by which we think of a straight line, whereby we see that, from its very nature, it must be the shortest line that there is or can be between the points. It is certain that we prove this proposition with regard to the straight line, as in fact, we do all other points in Geometry, by reasoning *a priori* and from the nature of the subject. We never resort to measurement; that method would be regarded as unscholarly and unsatisfactory. And we reason *a priori*, from the nature of the subject; and hence our conclusion, as the process has involved no accidental or mere circumstantial matter, is regarded as universal and absolutely true.

I cite another example both for the sake of proof and of illustration—the case of causation.

I have already spoken of this as having been used as a sort of test instance—*experimentum crucis*—between the two schools that differ so widely in regard to this matter. Locke, Mill and the men of that school, account for "the idea of cause," by reference to sensation alone; and as I have before remarked they reduce it to mere antecedence. Cousin, and those who agree with him on the other hand, claim "the idea of cause" as proof of either an *innate*, or at least an *a priori* idea "furnished by the reason," in its spontaneous activity. But as I have already remarked, on either theory there would be no difference between *antecedence* and *causation*; and it is not likely that any language would have the two words. On Locke's theory, we have, and can have only "the idea of antecedence," and on Cousin's theory, although we might "have both ideas," we could have no ground or means of distinguishing between cases. Nor could we apply the one word in the same cases, and the other in others. Nor could there be any cases to which both words might not, *so far as we have any means of discriminating*, be applied to one as well as to the other.

But there is a difference in the meaning and force of the two words. No one uses causation and antecedence indiscriminately. Everybody knows that there is a difference—that there may be antecedence without causation and—in a certain sense—causation without antecedence. How do we know the difference? Not by sensation alone—not by "sensation *and* "reflection" in Locke and Mill's sense of the word reflection. Not by any *innate* or *a priori* idea, for then there would be no means of discrimination.

I am inclined to think that M. de Biran, as stated by Cousin, who adopts his view, is right when he says, that "the "idea of cause is first derived from consciousness." Cousin's example is as good as any that has occurred to me. Suppose I am thinking of an air, and wish to hear it. In one case, I get up and go to the instrument and play it myself; in the other, some one in an adjoining room, unbeknown to me, and unseen by me, at that precise moment strikes up the air I was wishing to hear. In the one case I have the two elements, the thought of the music and the hearing of it; and in the other I have these two, with a third, which does not exist in the other, namely, *a consciousness of making the music*—which, in the last analysis, is resolved into a consciousness of myself as making the music, or as causing it, and so "the idea of "cause"—an element which is not contained in my consciousness of what occurred in the case of the music performed by another person, and in the adjoining room.

But "this idea" of cause, is the result of an insight into the phenomena. What I am conscious of is thinking, wishing, willing, *doing*, and hearing the music. No analysis will carry us back of these facts to a something that acted on me, so that in willing or doing, or in both together, I was only a second cause, a mere instrument. But even if there were, we should come to this ulterior something, as a *cause,* and as a cause *only.* It is not, and has not been cognized directly or immediately as an object, or by any objective properties whatever. Or in other words we know of nothing which *caused us* to will, or to do, in the premises. Hence we think of ourself as cause—and obtain the "idea" of cause—or causation, by the same process as in the case of sense-perception. I see this white paper, and then think of or have "the idea" of whiteness. I am conscious of willing and doing an act, and then think of myself as doing it, and by generalizing the fact, get the "idea" of cause.

Or again, I look out at my window and see, near by, a man trundling a wheel-barrow before him; and a little farther on up the hill, I see a horse drawing a wagon. I have no hesitation in saying that the horse *draws* the wagon. And I as unhesitatingly affirm that the man *pushes* the wheel-barrow; notwithstanding the barrow goes before the man, as the horse does before the wagon. In both cases I ascribe causality. I consider the horse as the cause in the one case, and the man in the other. But I do not see how, on Locke's theory, I could affirm that the man pushes the wheel-barrow any more than in the other case, I should say that the wagon pushes the horse. Mere antecedence is not enough. Suppose the horse and wagon were going down a very steep hill, I might find occasion to change my affirmation and say that the wagon pushes the horse, thus making the wagon the cause. Mere antecedence, whether in time or in space, is not of itself and alone, conclusive and final. Nay more, as I think I have shown, it could never of itself have suggested "the idea" of causation —or given rise to the word, or in fact, to any word that would mean more than mere antecedence.

It is possible that without the experience which, as de Biran and Cousin thought, gives rise to the "idea of cause," there might be an insight into the nature of the objects named, "horse," "wagon," "man," and "wheel-barrow," whereby we should affirm causation of the man and the horse, and deny it of the wagon and the wheel-barrow, and thus derive the "idea of cause" from phenomena in the external world. On this point, however, I prefer to express no opinion at present.

But in either case we see, think of, and so come to speak of, an agency, an efficiency which we call causation in some cases, which we do not see or ascribe in others.

I am unable to see how Mill and others, who advocate Locke's theory get over the difficulty here referred to. Like going to the moon, "*it is the first step that costs.*" When that has been successfully taken, the rest offer no difficulty. When a child has once *seen* a case of causation—once got the "idea" of a cause there is no difficulty in ascribing it, whenever there may be occasion, or disposition to do so. And it is very likely that with the "idea" once in the mind, we should be inclined to ascribe it, whenever we see a pretty uniform sequence. But how first get the "idea"? How first think of more than is apparent to sense-perception—the mere antecedence—in the first instance? Does it come by insight into the nature and relations of things in the outward world? Does it come from consciousness of volition and effort within? In either case there is more than these philosophers include in their enumeration and description of the sources of knowledge. And if so, why not extend this to other similar cases and solve the difficulty at once? The habitual association of which Mill makes so much account, needs something to begin with—some starting point which he has not furnished.

Now this act or fact of insight has not been, so far as I know and believe, distinctly recognized and described by any author or teacher of metaphysics. Doubtless it was included among the facts which led Plato to propose his theory of "ideas." I have no doubt it was one among the rest of those which Locke included, though he was not aware of it, in his somewhat comprehensive and ill-defined term "reflection." Nor have I any doubt that it was the presence and force of this element that led Kant to suggest his doctrine of *schemata*, Brown to propose his "relative suggestion," and Cousin to claim the reality of *a priori* ideas and the spontaneity of the reason. But no one of them pointed it out, or apparently, clearly saw it, as a distinct element of knowledge or "source of ideas." Like some one of the more recently discovered and widely diffused elements in Chemistry, it had always been present though not distinctly recognized—always influenced phenomena and alway given rise to theories and conjectures—which, satisfactory in some respects, involved consequences and doctrines which in others were untenable, if not absurd; while the distinct recognition of the new element makes all intelligible and consistent and satisfactory.

The word "*insight*" has been used by English writers for many years, undoubtedly; yet, I do not find that in any case it has been employed to denote precisely the form of mental activity, I have been speaking of. This was no doubt because, no one of those who have used it seems to have had any clear and distinct conception of what I mean, as a separate and original element in our mental activity. It differs widely from what the Germans do mean by their *Anschauung*—and the French by their *intuition.* They are both, as I think, forms of imagination or fancy. They are occupied with *things* or objects that might be seen; if they were present to the eye. Whereas insight, as I think is wholly occupied with *properties* — the properties and relations of things. I have no doubt, as I shall undertake to show bye-and-bye, that it furnishes the means by which we can *prove* the existence of objects that are unseen, and objects, moreover, which in their nature are invisible and have no sensible properties. But I do not think that any one of them, or any entity, whatever, is the immediate object of insight, unaccompanied by either sense-perception or consciousness. Insight goes along and coöperates with both. When I perceive an object, I have over and above the sight of it, some insight into its nature. When I am conscious of thinking, I have an insight into the nature of the process, so that I know that there can be no thinking where there is not something that thinks, and that beneath the phenomena there is an I that thinks, so that I can say *cogito ergo sum.* I think, therefore I am.

Again. In all classification there is an exercise of insight— and classification is essential to language itself. Language consists of words, a part of which are proper nouns or individual names, and another part consists of common nouns. Without this last there could be no language. But classification implies a discrimination of essential and accidental properties. Nay, even the distinction of two individual objects — *when not seen at the same time*—implies the recognition of some of the properties of each as only accidental, and others as essential or inseparable characteristics. And all classification, giving rise as it does to *common* nouns, denoting classes—*species* and *genera,* implies a like discrimination. But this *accidentalness* and this *essentialness,* are not sensible properties. They affect no one of the organs of the objective senses. They are purely matter of insight. They are not in all cases distinguished at first sight. It may require time and reflection to appreciate them. But we do distinguish and discriminate them. And we distinguish individual objects by them. And by them too, we arrange all objects of thought into these subordinate classes, on which all reasoning and all language as well depends.

I have not, however, yet stated what I believe to be the greatest and most prevailing function of this faculty of insight. I believe it to be the basis or organ of all those elementary axioms which underlie all science, and all branches of knowledge; and which we call intuitive or self-evident. They are what Kant called, as I have explained in a preceding Lecture, "Analytic Judgments, *a priori*." Surely there is something more in these than mere sense-perception. And I cannot see how ideas, whether innate, *a priori*, or obtained in any other way, can help the matter.

There is an orange on the table before me. I *see* that it is round, redish, somewhat hard, and rather rough in its surface, I can *imagine* that its color will change, that its form will deliquesce, or its surface become smooth as polished marble; though I do not expect any of these changes. But it is also extended, and I *know* that it is divisible, and I *know* too, that these two properties cannot disappear. It may be condensed by pressure until it will have the density of platinum or of a diamond. It may become expanded for aught I know, until its rarity will be as great as that of hydrogen, or any other gas of less specific gravity, if there be one. But yet it will be extended, with a greater or less expansion of surface; and so long as it is extended it will be divisible. No change can deliver it or relieve it of these properties. Only annihilation can do that; and then it is no longer an orange; it has become nothing, it has no properties, not even extension.

Now, manifestly, here are two classes of properties which the orange is supposed to possess, and there are two classes of propositions which we affirm concerning it. Properties of the one class can be changed the one into the other, or totally disappear, as the color in the dark, or the hardness by evaporation; and our affirmation of them makes what we call contingent matter—synthetic *a posteriori*. And the other properties, though they may be changed in degree as extension, divisibility, etc., can not be changed in kind or become extinct, so long as the object itself remains; and the affirmation of these properties constitutes what we call necessary matter. And so far as we have yet considered it, it is analytic *a priori*.

Nor is this all. I not only know of the orange, that it is extended and divisible, but I know the same, and that too, without any observation, of any and every piece of matter, whether mass or molecule, that actually exists. I know it, as I say, without any observation, experience or testimony concerning it. It belongs to its very nature, and I know by insight into its nature as a material object, that whatever else it may be, and wherever else it may be, it is extended and divisible; extended in fact, and divisible in theory; divisible if we have the power and means to divide it.

To say that we cannot separate "the idea of extension from the idea of material substance," as philosophers of the ideal school do, does not express the thought. It is not, with me, a question of "*ideas*" or of "*separation*" at all—but a question of the nature of matter, and pertains equally to any material substance whatever, totally independent of all other properties, considerations or conditions. And to say, as writers of the sensational school do, that my inability to think of matter without extension, and of extension without divisibility, is merely a habit that has grown up from the frequent and unvarying perception of them together, comes utterly short of explaining the confidence I feel in the certainty of the truth of my assertion. I have never actually and really perceived either *extension* or *divisibility* or their "ideas," any more than I have perceived the "shortestness" of the straight line. And I can no more perceive the one than the other. Hence I cannot understand how my confidence can have come, as Mill holds that it does, from the frequency and constant recurrence of that which can never have occurred at all.

The remark I have thus made and illustrated with regard to the primary axioms in necessary matter, extends to all those propositions that we are accustomed to call "self-evident." They are of such a nature that the truth of the propositions is evident to insight as soon as we understand the nature of the subject and the meaning of the predicate, we affirm of it; just as in all our primary judgments in contingent matter, the truth of the assertion is apparent as soon as we *see* or *perceive* the object and know the meaning of the predicate. This paper is white. I need only to see the paper and to know what the word "white" means, to assent to the proposition; *knowing* that it is true. But when we say that a straight line is the shortest possible line between two points, I do not need to *see* the line or anything else--probably no mere line could be *seen* at all—but only to conceive of it. I can not even imagine it. But I can conceive of it, know what it is; and as soon as I do this, I know that there can be no shorter line between the same limiting points.

With such axioms all knowledge begins. They are first in the logical order, though not, as I think, in any case, the first in the chronological order ; we see objects first, and before we *see into* them. We are conscious of mental states, before we have, or can have, any insight into their nature. But with perception and consciousness there comes insight ; and with reflection this same function continues. We soon evolve, and and state explicitly, certain fundamental and self-evident axioms ; such as are stated usually at the outset in any treatise of Geometry ; and such as are implied, and constantly assumed, in the prosecution and teaching of any science, or branch of knowledge whatever.

This insight into the meaning of propositions and into the nature of things, accompanies and enters into every act of reasoning, and every act of understanding and comprehension, we ever perform. It makes all the difference between the man of wisdom and of genius on the one hand, and the merest idiot —not at all above the brutes in the scale of intelligence, on the other. It is by it and because of it that *we* understand, and it is because of the want of it that *they* can not.

It is well to take note again of test words which Cousin has proposed. They are not mere inventions of his own. They are the accumulation of centuries of controversy. The schoolmen had proposed some of them, Locke suggested others, and I believe that Cousin himself added to the list a few of his own selection. His list is as follows : "Space," "Time," "The Infinite," "Personal Identity," "Substance," "Cause," "Good and Evil."

Of these "time" and "space" denote no real or substantial objects—nor yet the objectified properties, relations or modes of objects. They are pure creations of fancy—very useful, nay indispensable, to science and to speech, doubtless. But they are pure creations of fancy nevertheless ; and hence they imply neither sensation, nor insight, nor yet "ideas" as ontological realities; but only acts of fancy or imagination. They are not causes, they are never imagined as real agents or forces; and are spoken of as objects and agents only by a recognized and admitted figure of speech.

The terms "infinite" and "substance" belong to another category. They are but etymological compounds, and imply only a process of word-making, of which any person living is capable. We doubtless get "finite" from our experience of objects; they exist for a while or for a space, and then come to an end, or rather they cease to exist. We call that, an end and *finis*—and so we call them finite or end-having. But we can *suppose* something not having an end: we can suppose it, I say, though we cannot imagine it; and I am inclined to think that we can prove that nothing that is extended, either in space or time, can be without an end also. But when we have supposed it, we can easily put before the adjective *finite* the negative particle "in," and we have the word "infinite." But what does it mean? It is easy to say that it means "without limits." But without limits is a negative term, and by one of the first and most fundamental laws of Logic, negative terms affirm nothing. Hence *their* origin implies neither sensation, "ideas," nor yet insight—but only etymological construction, mere word manufacture.

The word "substance," however, will hardly be regarded as a negative term. Nor does its use, in several of its acceptations or senses, require any explanation here. They involve no difficulty. And if there had been no use of the word besides them, it never would have been cited as an example or test in this controversy. We call any object a substance, when we wish to denote it as a reality and have no special reference to its accidental modes and properties. In this sense the pen, the paper, the book, etc., are each and all substances.

Again we call chemical or mineral matters substances—as when we say iron is a substance, limestone another, and so on ; notwithstanding there may be a great many objects that are made of these substances, and into which they are divided.

But in the sense in which metaphysicians use the word substance—and that is the only one that puzzles us—it denotes a something that has no properties, something that underlies, or under*stands*, rather, all properties, something that would be left if we should take all the properties away. Of course, there is no such thing ; the word is a mere etymological compound denoting the supposed result of an impossible process.

"Personal Identity" cannot be derived from sensation alone —for leaving out of account now the word "identity," we can have no "idea" of person—can not even think of it, or in any way have the thought of it, as part of our knowledge, except by insight. We penetrate through the phenomena that are apparent in consciousness ; and see that below thought—and before it, there is a something that thinks. And this something, we call the person ; or we may call it by any other word —the name is unimportant. But the word as well as the thing, do undoubtedly, imply something besides, and more than sensation, and mere sense-perception. The mere fact that the person or self has no sensible properties is proof of this.

But I do not readily see how "personal identity" can be of more importance than mere personality, in such a controversy as this. Identity, I think, implies not a sensation or an "idea" or mere insight even, but a judgment and a comparison, as well. Nay, it implies more. It implies some accepted criterion of identity. We have all heard of the vexed question about the identity of the boy's jack-knife—which had lost first the blade, then the handle, and finally the spring, and had

had each and all of these parts replaced as soon as they were gone. The whole difficulty results from the want of a criterion or standard of identity in the case.

Of the word "cause" I have said all that the occasion calls for. I think it an unanswerable refutation of Locke's theory; and of the whole doctrine and system of philosophy that would derive *all* our knowledge from sensation alone, without either "ideas" or insight. But for reasons already given, I do not see how it can prove the reality of ideas—or the ideal theory of the origin of knowledge in any of the forms it has assumed—or in any form it can assume.

The terms "good" and "evil," as distinct from pleasant and painful, do indeed imply, as Cousin has so eloquently urged, something more than sense-perception; just as the word "cause," as something more than mere antecedence, implies such an element of knowledge. But I do not see how they imply the reality of "ideas" any more than any and every other adjective, or abstract term derived from an adjective. Nor has Cousin shown us how this is to be inferred. It is in deed a "survival" of the old Platonic notion—that the *properties* of objects are realities, the only realities; that they are ideas, and are the very essence of the objects to which they are attached. On this theory, names for these properties do imply the properties, which are ideas, and of course, therefore, ideas themselves. But the words "good" and "evil" imply these ideas no more than any other adjectives that we may use to denote the qualities of objects or acts.

In another, and an important sense, however, these words do imply something more than sensation. And in this respect they differ from other adjectives. They denote no *sensible* properties, as do for instance the adjectives "hard" "red" "sweet" "bitter," etc. Hence they imply something besides mere sense-perception for their origin as representatives or expressions of a part of our knowledge. What they require, however, is not, as I think, any "ideas," but only an insight into the nature of the acts which we call good or bad.

The objections to the sensational theory of the origin of knowledge, regarded as exclusive of all other sources or means are,

1st. The theory does not, in any of its forms, modifications, or statements, account for that part of our knowledge which is expressed by (1) such adjectives as I have called metaphysical—such as represent no sensible quality—as "shortest" "causal," etc., or (2) by such names as denote real things, which yet can not have been cognized by sense-perception as "person," "mind," etc. These words are found in all languages. They are neither abstract nor negative. They are both positive and concrete; they denote objects which are known as causes, if not by objective properties also.

2d. The theory does not, in any of its statements or modifications, account for the certainty or confidence which we certainly feel in the analytic *a priori* propositions—the axioms and self-evident propositions, which underlie all knowledge and constitute, in fact, the Major Premises—to all reasoning, even in the *a posteriori* sciences. We call them self-evident because we see their truth as soon as we understand or comprehend the meaning of their terms. They need no proof, no intervention of a Middle Term. And, in fact, from their very nature, they admit of none. The first principles or premises of reasoning, can not be the result of any previous process of reasoning. Nor can they, in fact, be *proved* by reasoning, though they can be *tested* as we shall show in the next Lecture, by the indirect method.

3d. And finally, it leads to Nominalism, and its inevitable consequences, materialism and atheism. It is not only that it *fails* to account for certain words, or that it does not explain them, and their existence and use in all human languages. It is active in the negative way as well. It teaches that there are and can be no entities, no realities, substances and causes that are not material and that do not have sensible properties. Not only does the theory fail to prove their existence and account for the origin of the words that denote such objects, but it gives us, as irrefutable and unquestionable, the data, on which, by the use of the principle of identity and contradiction, we can prove that there are no such things as realities, and show that their very supposition involves a contradiction of terms. It is just as if we admit that twice two are five; we can render any proposition in mathematics absurd, and throw confusion, uncertainty and disagreement into all the transactions of life. We can escape these consequences only by showing that the fundamental principle, the seminal fact, is absurd. There is a means of knowledge besides sense-perception.

The objections to the idealistic theory, in whatever form, and under whatever modifications it has been presented, are,

1st. It assumes the existence of ideas, as something more than mere states of the mind, mere modes or forms of thought. If they are no more than *states of* the mind, they explain nothing; they account for nothing pertinent to the question. Any resort to them is but saying that we think so and so, because we *do* think so and so. Instead of accounting for the phenomena they only state and affirm their existence in other terms, with another form of phraseology. If ideas are anything more than mere thoughts, their reality as such has not been proved. Nay, I suppose it will be admitted that they have no such existence, whenever attention is called to the point. And in fact, I presume that I could cite words that imply as much, from nearly or quite every philosopher who has written on the subject from Plato down to our times.

2d. But waiving this objection, and admitting the reality of ideas for the present, it does not appear how they are a source of knowledge, or a ground of certainty. Whence come they? What assurance have we that they represent things? Or rather, what ground have we for such assurance? If we say they come from God and with Cousin, that they are "the essence of God," His existence is assumed in the assertion and we rest all knowledge on an act of faith in Him. Now I have no objection to the exercise of faith. Nay, I believe in it; but to rest *knowledge* upon it, and make it the cornerstone and foundation of *knowledge*, is to vacate the term knowledge of its characteristic and distinctive meaning. What we know compels us to believe in something that we do not know.

3d. As the attempt to account for all Knowledge, by reference to sense-perception alone, has led to mere *Nominalism*, so on the other hand, it is customary to speak of the theory that derives it from ideas alone, as leading to Realism.* But it seems to me that Idealism is rather a step in the progress of Realism, than its origin and cause. Idealists *begin* with the objectification of abstractions. They make of thought, a reality, and call it ideas. Hence what is called Realism is actually begun before idealism is possible. Realism leads to idealism rather than the reverse.

*I call it "*Realism*" in accordance with the common usage. But it seems to me that I am more truly a realist and more of a realist than they. They are called realists because they regard as real, mere unsubstantial nonentities. My claim is based on the fact that I would limit all knowledge and all that is to be regarded as such, to substantial realities.

It is also customary to speak of Pantheism as the characteristic outcome and practical *reductio ad absurdum* of Idealism. But it seems to me that our modern physicists—by objectifying mere properties, and modes of action, and treating them as forces and real causes, have reached a materialism that is about as bald and lifeless, as that of the Nominalists and Pantheists themselves, taking, as they do, the other extreme as a starting point.

This whole controversy concerning the origin and nature of knowledge has been, from the very beginning, embarrassed, by this innate, and apparently unconquerable tendency to objectify mere modes and properties—neglecting the substantial things in nature, and treating their modes and properties as realities. This is eminently conspicuous in Cousin's Review of Locke's Psychology. He treats "time" and "space" as his strongest points. He elaborates the part of his argument that is based on them, with the utmost care and zest. It does not appear to have occurred to him that any body ever did, or ever could, doubt the substantial reality of these assumed entities. And, if not, his argument was complete—his refutation overwhelming; though I do not see how it could prove the reality of ideas.

But I think that the function of insight, when duly considered, answers all the demands and conditions of the problem. It certainly supplies, or rather, more properly speaking, it accounts for, all the elements of knowledge that sensationalism has proved itself incompetent to account for. It assumes nothing, and is unlike the theory of ideas in this respect. It is, undoubtedly, a real mental act. All men understand it. All men speak of getting an insight into a thing, and there is no man that speaks the English language, so ignorant that he will not understand you when you so use the word. You refer to something that he is conscious of, as having occurred in his own experience. He may not be aware that he is *all* the time getting an insight; or that he is "seeing into" things every time he sees anything; draws any inferences from a principle, or makes any application of a rule. But he is conscious of many an hour of hard study, of intense thought, when what he is trying to do, and the only thing that occasions any effort in the doing, is the seeing into or getting an insight into something that he does not at once and easily understand.

And this is insight; it is the leading characteristic of all intelligence; it furnishes an element in all knowledge. It enables us to reason from the seen to the unseen, and to draw clearly and sharply the line of distinction that marks off knowledge and certainty on the one hand, from the domain of mere opinion, and the still more etherial domain of faith, on the other. It constitutes the "good sense" of the great mass of mankind. It sharpens into "the tact" of the successful man of the world, it grows brilliant in the man of "genius," it guides the imagination of the artist and the artizan so that the products of their labor are objects of beauty and not mere monstrosities. And combined with sentiment, and the result of that experience which comes from the exercise of faith, it gives the highest tone, and the finest trait to that spirituality of character, which triumphs over things material and temporal, and is the sure hope and fruition of the presence and favor of God, both here and hereafter.

LECTURE V.

THE TEST OF TRUTH.

The next of the three great questions which we have reserved for consideration, is that which relates to the test and limit of absolute truth—fixing the border line that divides off truth and knowledge, from mere opinion and the domain of faith.

The admitted facts, that "the senses deceive us," and that "there can be no science of the variable," constituted the leading features in the problem, which Plato set himself to solve; and to solve which he proposed his theory of ideas. The same problem led Aristotle to the composition of most or all of his Logical Treatises; and it occupied a large share of the attention of every speculator from the time of Zeno, the Eleatic, to the close of the Alexandrian period.

The same question was the leading object alike with Descartes and Locke, with Leibintz and Bacon, with Reid and Brown, with Kant and Cousin. Sir William Hamilton and John Stuart Mill, each had a theory of his own on the subject, and the discussion of it has entered largely into the writings and speculations of every one who has either done, or aimed to do, any original thinking, within the domain of metaphysics. And yet the question is unsettled.

The schoolmen had held that it "is impossible for the same thing to be and not to be at the same time." Leibintz, as we have seen, formulated and expressed the same doctrine in what has generally been called since his time, the principle of identity and contradiction. The other great principle of knowledge or ground of affirmation he stated as the principle of sufficient cause.

Now, the fundamental difference between these two—in relation to the assertions, or the doctrines that can be based upon them respectively, in this; whatever is true or can be affirmed on the principle of Identity, is necessarily and absolutely true, independent of times, circumstances, conditions and places, the truth of the affirmation being founded in the very nature of the subject; while whatever is affirmed on the ground of sufficient cause, is only conditionally and contingently true. Its truth depends upon the will, the intention, or the activity, at least, of the agent or cause that produced it. There is, therefore a reason for saying that the propositions of the first kind express *truths*; while those of the latter kind express only *facts* or *events*. To the former there can be no exceptions; we cannot imagine one, nor even suppose one; if by supposing it we imply any belief in its reality or possibility, anything more than the mere putting together of words in a proposition which are self-contradicting. In this sense, we can *suppose*, that is, speak of, two straight lines as enclosing a space, but not with the belief that they do, or can by any possibility enclose a space.

But with regard to the assertions or "truths," that rest on the principle of Sufficient cause, we not only can suppose and imagine exceptions; we know that, for the most part, exceptions do occur, and we can imagine the whole law or truth to be reversed. Thus it is a truth of this kind, commonly accepted, that every piece of matter attracts every other piece of matter, with an intensity proportional to its mass, and inversely as the square of the distance between them. But we can imagine exceptions to this rule or law. We can even imagine it reversed, so that these masses and molecules will repel, instead of attracting one another. It is indeed true that if this were the case, it would make or require a change in almost, if not quite all of our cosmical laws, and the system of the material universe dependent upon them. But we can even imagine the material universe as not existing. Most of us believe in a time before it existed, and of a time when it shall have ceased to exist.

The difference then, is a fundamental one, and it becomes a question of the utmost importance, how far does the principle of identity and contradiction extend.

We sometimes speak of them as two, and at others as one —the only difference is that if the proposition is true, it rests on the principle of identity; and if false it can be tested by that of contradiction. Or in other words, if the proposition be true, it can be reduced to the form, A is A, and if false it can be reduced to the form, some A is not A, that is, in the old phraseology of the scholastics, if it is true, so that A is A, it cannot be possible that any of A is not A. Or if All A are A, it cannot be true that some A are not A.

It is customary to add by an express statement, what is clearly implied in the foregoing, namely, that the use of the predicate must be taken and understood in reference to the same time and the same relations; thus a man may be both father and son, though the words are contradictory, father to one person, and a son to another. A man may be both sick and well; sick at one time and well at another. Or a man may be tall when compared with a short race of men, and yet spoken of as a short man if compared with a race much taller than he is.

We have seen that Kant, while recognizing the principle of identity and contradiction, thought that it could be applied to only the analytic *a priori* propositions. And this virtually restricted it to mere definitions. And, if so, of course, it was no means or ground of *knowledge* at all; since in knowing that an object is, whatever may be our means of knowledge, we know all of it that we can know by its definition, all that we can really express in a definition. In fact, a definition is but the expansion and expression of the idea, or conception, which, to use the language of those schools,—we form of the object in the very act of cognizing it, or understanding what it is. I have a conception of a plane figure. I call it a triangle. I say it has three sides. In each of these three mental stages or acts, there is just the same amount of knowledge; and neither the giving the name, nor the affirmation of three-sidedness, increases the knowledge there was in the conception, before naming the object or making the affirmation concerning it. In case, however, an assertion increases our knowledge, or affirms anything concerning the object that was "not contained in the mere conception of it," the proposition becomes synthetic. Thus, if I say the triangle has three sides, the proposition is analytic—but if I say it *exists*, the proposition is synthetic. and may call for proof.

We all admit that the contradictory of any real or logical definition is a contradiction in terms; and so involves an ontological absurdity—a something that is nothing, and can not exist or be real as an entity, or a law or a truth anywhere. If we define a triangle as a three-sided figure, and then speak of a triangle that has not three sides, we have a case in point. We do not need to make any words about it, and are not likely to make any.

But no predicate, that is not obviously involved in the very conception of the object denoted by the subject of the proposition, can be thus affirmed in a definition or included within the scope which Kant would allow to the principle of indentity and contradiction. Hence, to speak of anything and say "it exists," would transcend this scope—since its existence is not implied in the conception of anything. We can imagine or suppose it to exist, even when we know that it does not. Hence we are left, not only to a perfect blank with regard to the whole sphere of ontology; but we are left also without any fundamental principles of science, the very first Premises for induction, or any certainty in the domain of knowledge anywhere.

I think that Kant made his fatal admission, chiefly because he did not take time to consider, or perhaps, because there had not been so much done then as now, to show what the principle really means, and how it may be applied.

There is, indeed, a broad difference between the principle of identity and contradiction, and the method of applying it. The principle is obvious to the insight of all men. It needs no proof. It is assented to by all persons as soon as it is understood. And so, too, its *application* to all merely analytic propositions, is obvious and easy, so that we never ask to see it applied, or to have the proposition reduced to the form in which its application is obvious. We see it, and are content with seeing it. We do not ask to have its application displayed.

And here our work must begin. We say all triangles have three sides. We see at once, that if any figure has not three sides it is not a triangle, whatever else it may be. And here we ordinarily stop. We have not reduced the proposition to the form of a contradiction in terms; *but we see that it contains one*, just as an algebraist, from the formula, $x^2+8x+16=64$, sees that $x=4$, without going through the operation of solving the equation. Nevertheless, as truly as in the algebraic example, there is a process of solution and resolution whereby $x^2+8x+16$ can be brought into the form $x+4$, without changing the value of a single term, letter or figure, in the original formula, so truly can the proposition "a triangle has three sides," be brought to the form A is A—that is, to a proposition, in which both subject and predicate are one and the same. Or if the proposition is false it can be brought to the form Some A is not A ; on what has been explained as the principle of contradiction.

Now that the principle of identity and contradiction does extend beyond the mere analytic propositions, the mere logical definitions, I think can be made perfectly obvious, without considering at all how it is to be applied. The mode of applying it is indeed a more difficult matter ; and I think I might accomplish all I need to do in this connection, by showing the applicability of the principle without going into the method of applying it at all ; although I propose to make some suggestions on this subject before I close this Lecture.

Let us see what the principle really is. It has been expressed as I have said in the form "a thing can not be, and not be at the same time." But in a more general form it is, that nothing can exist in a manner, mode or form, which is inconsistent with, or contradicts its very nature. If *three-sidedness* is of the nature or essence of a triangle, there can be nothing, figure or object, that is triangular and not three-sided. If extension is of the very nature and essence of matter, there can be no piece of matter, mass or molecule, that is not extended. And if extension implies divisibility, there can be no piece of matter which is not also divisible. Hence if one says, this triangle has not three sides, we do not hesitate to say, you are mistaken, it may be something else—but a triangle it certainly is not. And for the most part we go no farther. No one asks or desires, that we should; we have done what is required in all *demonstration.* We have taken the last step that is needed or expected. We have brought the truth to the insight of the hearer. He sees it, and is content. He asks no more; and more would be tedious and unnecessary, if not an unendurable prolixity, and an insult to his understanding. It is, however, but one step more to say, if it were so we should have a "a triangle that is not a triangle," or "a triangle that is not triangular—a three-sided figure that is not three-sided.

Such a contradiction cannot occur in necessary matter. It can occur only in that part of the natural sciences where a generalization is based on prominent properties, which, however, may not be of the essence and nature of the subject. We have an example in the case of "white black birds." That is, the animals are called *black* birds, though the blackness is not essential. It may be, and probably is, a prevalent color; but it is not the differentia of the species. A bird may be white and be a "black bird" nevertheless.

Now, suppose we go one step farther. All admit that a plane figure that has not three sides, is not a triangle; this would be, if it were contradicted, the contradiction of an analytic proposition. Hence we say if the figure has not three sides it is not a triangle. But suppose we go one step farther and say, "the sum of the angles in any triangle, is equal to two right angles." This would be a synthetic proposition. Thousands know what a triangle is, without knowing this property of triangles. I suppose we can all recollect the time when we had to learn it, with more or less of labor. But when we had learned it, and had really mastered the demonstration by which it is proved, not only seen into it, but "*seen through*" it, it became a matter of necessary truth, as much so as the original definition or axiom had been. And we had come to know as fully after that demonstration that if the angles of any plane figure bounded by straight lines, are not equal to two right angles, the figure is not a triangle, as we did, or could have done, when the assertion was made that it had not three sides, or had not just three angles, and neither more nor less.

But, if this be true, and I presume no one will doubt or dispute it, then the synthetic proposition of the equality of the angles to two right angles, is as much and as truly founded in the very nature and essence of the triangle, as its definition; and the one as truly rests upon the principles of identity and contradiction as the other. The only difference is in the method of applying the principle. But if the principle applies to the case, there must be a way of applying it; though possibly it may not yet have been found out and stated to the world. There was a time when the method of solving cubic equations had not been found out, and yet, even then, men must have known that for any complete cube there must be some way of finding its root. Even to-day, some mathematicians believe there is a way of solving equations of the fifth degree, although no one knows how it can be done.

We ought not, however, to stop here with our illustrations. I select my next example on grounds which are somewhat peculiar to myself. It is an elementary doctrine in plane Trigonometry, that the sines of the several angles in any triangle are to each other as the sides opposite these angles are respectively. The doctrine of the equality of the angles to two right angles was easily seen by me, but this matter with regard to the ratios of sines and opposite sides *seemed* at first thought impossible. At any rate, it was far more difficult to comprehend than the other. And I found great difficulty in *realizing* its truth after I had mastered the demonstration ; so that to *me* it was most emphatically synthetic. And yet, when once mastered it became as self-evident as either of the others I have named. And I was as thoroughly sure and confident that if in any case this ratio or proportion did not hold true, the figure, whatever else it might be, could not be a plane triangle. The truth as completely rested on the principle of identity and contradiction as the definition of the triangle itself. And, representing the angles by the small letters, *a*, *b*, etc., and the opposite sides by the corresponding capitals, we have the proportion, sin. *a* : sin. *b* : : A : B. And, if in any case we should find that the equation is not true, we should as unhesitatingly, and for the same reason declare, the figure not to be a plane triangle, as if we had found that it had not three sides or three angular corners.

What I have thus said of the two last named truths in regard to triangles, extends to every proposition in Mathematics, every doctrine that the Mathematician ever affirms, so long as he confines himself to his appropriate sphere of quantity and form only. They are synthetic ; they, most of them, at least, increase his knowledge ; they extend his understanding, and the scope of his comprehension ; they are not evident at first sight, as the many, long, and weary hours of labor which they cost him, abundantly attest. But he begins with definitions and self-evident axioms ; proceeds by steps, each one of which, is, or must be made, self-evident, before he can proceed any farther ; and they lead to results which are as truly founded in the nature of the subject of his investigations, and as truly based on the principle of identity and contradiction, as the first axioms—the self-evident analytic propositions he started with.

For the sake of one or two more illustrations—and it seems to me important that this point should be well illustrated—we will take the following. In the pursuit of Analytic Geometry, we soon find that the equation $x^2+y^2=R^2$, is one of the many equations of the circle. If now, a mathematician should find in any line, a point, whose coördinates are not exactly given by this equation, he would know that that line is not a circle, as truly as if he knew that some of its radii, were not equal to others.

Or, if in pursuing the Calculus, he comes to the equation $dx=ydy$ divided by the square root of($2ry-y^2$,) as an expression of the cycloid, and yet, should find that dy does not become zero whenever y becomes equal to either zero or $2r$, he would know that the curve, whatever else it might be, could not be a cycloid. These doctrines or facts have become as obvious to him, and in a certain sense, as *self*-evident as the first axioms of his Geometry, or his Algebra. They are as obvious to his insight, as soon as he sees into them, or sees through them, as the diagrams or the letters he uses in expressing the equations that represent them, are to his sight.

The entire process of "indirect proof," as it is called, rests on this principle. It furnishes another illustration of it, an illustration too, that is, in some respects better than any we have considered. It introduces us to the consideration of another principle of reasoning, known technically as the principle of the *Excluded Middle.*

Take as an example the ordinary proof of the proposition

that "a straight line let fall from any given point, upon another straight line so as to make a right angle with it, is the shortest line that can be drawn from that point to the line." The method of proof usually begins by supposing that some other line is shorter than the one drawn from the point perpendicularly to the line, and arrives at the conclusion that the assertion that any other line is shorter than the one that is drawn perpendicularly, implies that there is a line *which is shorter than the shortest.* But "shorter than the shortest" is a contradiction in terms. The contradiction is obvious to insight; although the proposition may not have been put into the form where the contradiction is obvious to inspection. And, we infer, that if the proposition which asserts that any other line than the perpendicular is shorter than it, is absurd—*it is so because it involves a contradiction in terms,* and its contradictory—"the perpendicular line is the shortest"—is true by Excluded Middle, that is, by virtue of a contradictory apposition between them. The principle merely implies that there is no other proposition in the same terms, however diffierent in quantity or quality, that can be true, while both of these are false.

I think it worth while for the sake of the completeness of the statement of the subject, to go a little farther and call attention to one aspect more of the case.

All language is based on a classification of the objects denoted by the terms of a proposition. Triangles, for example, are but one *species* of the proximate genus, plane figures. And every *affirmative* proposition asserts either the ontological identity of the subject and predicate, as A is A,—or that the subject is an individual or a class, in the higher class *denoted* by the predicate, if it be a noun; or *connoted* by it if it be an adjective, as "horses are quadrupeds," "horses are useful," etc.

In the same way a negative proposition excludes the subject from the class denoted by the predicate, as "birds are not mammals." When, therefore, we apply the principle of identity and contradiction, I get the result A is not A, we do not infer that A is no-thing, and does not denote any real or possible entity, but only that it cannot be in the species to which the proposition referred it. A "triangle" without three sides, cannot be in the species triangle ; it may be a rectangle, etc. That is, it may be a plane figure of another species, but not a triangle.

Now, whether we can in all cases reduce the doctrines, or rather the propositions in which they are stated, to the form that exhibits an identity of terms, or a contradiction in terms, is a question of our ability, and of our *present* ability and attainments in this matter ; and not at all a question as to whether the principle of identity and contradiction, underlies and serves as a basis to them or not. We have seen, I think, that it does sustain this relation to them ; that every mathematician so regards the matter, and that he acts upon it, and never asserts or assents to a proposition, until he has *seen* this underlying principle, this basis of truth. And if, at present, we can not reduce the equation, or proposition to that form, we are in the same relation to the matter as all were in regard to the methods of solving the higher equations before they were discovered ; just where we ourselves were, when we began our Algebra, and before we had learned how to solve our quadratic and cubic equations.

I do not know that any effort was ever made to show the process of this resolution until the publication of my "*Introduction to Metaphysics and the History of Philosophy,*" in 1872. The method there presented is, in many respects, analogous to

Algebra. That science, or art, perhaps we should rather call it, consists in ways and rules for the transformation of equations, performing operations upon them, and making changes in their terms, so that the value of the unknown quantity may be found, or the relation of one term to another may be made obvious to sight. So in this case, the process consists in changing the form of expression, and substituting certain words for others, until the proposition comes to exhibit the truth which had all along been concealed, though implied, in its previous form.

But to explain and apply the process is, as I have said, quite another affair. And yet, undoubtedly, it can be done. To take the simplest case and give an idea of the process, we will select an example from the science of numbers. Suppose we have the equation in figures $1+2=3$. It is manifest that 2 may be written $1+1$, and 3 may be written $1+1+1$. Now, putting the equation into the new form which we have found to be practicable without changing the value of its terms, we have $1+1+1=1+1+1$, the two members are identical. Hence we may call them by the same name, and have A is A, or three is three. And it will make no difference what A denotes, so long as we can be perfectly sure that it denotes precisely the same thing in both places as subject and as predicate.

If any one doubts or hesitates at either of these steps, we must do as we always do elsewhere, reduce it to its more elementary forms, if it has any, and if not, illustrate and explain, until the doubter sees, or rather, sees *into* its truth. Do you ask what we shall do, if after all he *don't* see it, or *won't* see it? I hardly know what to say. One thing is certain however, we are not supposed to be dealing with perversity, or trying to overcome obstinacy—that belongs to the Rhetorician. We are enacting only the *role* of the logician and the philosopher. So too, there are undoubtedly, various degrees of quickness and penetration of insight. I have seen boys to whom, one-half at least, of the propositions in plane Geometry were so obviously true that they needed no demonstration or proof. They saw *into* them, at once, and saw through them too, as soon as they saw them at all. The propositions were as self-evident as the axioms they began with. And then, too, I have seen boys who apparently could not learn much of mathematics, whether Geometry or Algebra, except as the saying is, by heart; in which case they did not *understand* it at all. But I never knew that anybody had doubted or denied the truth of mathematics on that account. But more than this, I believe, and I think I both can demonstrate, and have demonstrated in practice, the doctrine, that while all the synthetic proposition, *a priori*, can be tested by the principle of identity, the analytical propositions—even the axioms and so-called self-evident truths can be tested—I do not say *proved*—by the same principle, under its negative form, as the principle of contradiction. Thus, suppose one says $1+2$ is not equal to 3, then, of course, it is equal to some other number, say 4, and we have the equation, $1+2=4$. Resorting to the process before used, we get for $1+2$, $1+1+1$, which we call A or three, then for 4 we get $1+1+1+1$, which is evidently not A, or not three, and we have A is not A, or three are not three.

Or take the axiom "the whole is equal to the sum of the parts." It is allowable for all the purposes of mathematics, though not always elsewhere, to say that "the whole *is* the sum of the parts" and "the sum of the parts is the whole." The two terms of the proposition denote the same thing; and therefore, they may be used (in mathematics) the one for the other. They may even replace one another, and be predicated of each other in an identical proposition. This I say, is always true in mathematics, but not necessarily or even usually so elsewhere. In ontology the statement implies the fallacy of divisions and composition. All the members—or parts of a committee, are not the committee, nor yet equal to it, except when they are assembled together, organized and acting as a Committee.

I have thus far spoken only of mathematical truths and have drawn all my illustrations and proofs from that source. But there is another great department of truth ; and if our principle of identity and contradiction does not carry us into that, it is of comparatively little use to us.

Mathematics deals with objects irrespective of their individual characteristics ; it deals with them as unites only. Ontology, on the other hand, deals with them as individuals ; and as individuals, they must be distinguished from one another by essential properties, and included in species and genera. Hence, they must have essentia, differentia and accidents, separable and inseparable. And all reasoning concerning them must be based on their properties, while in mathematics, the properties are never taken into account.

Again, mathematics neither proves nor assumes the *existence* and reality of anything. It deals purely with hypotheses, and the conditions and laws under which objects *as individuals may exist and act.* It does not assume that there is a triangle or any object in triangular form, actually in existence anywhere. It only says, that if there is such an object it must have three sides, "the sum of its angles must be equal to two right angles," and the sines of any two of its angles must bear a constant ratio to their corresponding opposite sides, etc.

But in ontology, the very first question in the chronological order of knowledge is, "does anything exist?" Is there a subjective reality that thinks and perceives? Is there any outward object, any external reality that is perceived and thought about? Can any affirmation with regard to the existence and relations of such objects be based upon or tested by the principles of identity and contradiction?

This is really the question of practical importance. It is the question that is fundamental to all philosophy, whether physical or metaphysical. And yet it is regarded as purely a metaphysical question, a question of transcendental Logic.

Let us take for example the words "perceive" and "imagine." "I perceive the table" before me. This is ordinarily understood to imply the objective reality of the table, as well as the subjective reality of myself, the perceiving agent. Again, "I imagine a man crossing the street." This does not imply that I see him—does not imply that there is any man crossing the streets, nor in fact, that there is any man or any street, anywhere. The assertion is purely subjective; it affirms something with regard to myself, what I am doing or thinking about. But it neither affirms nor (perhaps), implies anything with regard to anybody or anything else; for I can imagine the man crossing the street, even if there is neither street to be crossed, nor a man to cross it.

Doubtless, there is an important difference between imagination and conception, the difference I think is this; in imagination, we think of things such as might be seen and felt, by their sensible properties. We apply the word conception rather to objects that have no sensible properties, as to classes, species and genera. We may imagine the individual, but we conceive of the class, the species or the genus. Hence, we can conceive of what we can not imagine.

But between perception and imagination there is this further difference. The one, perception, is derived from a transitive verb, and the other from a verb which is active only and not transitive. If I say "I imagine," I state a fact with regard to my own mental condition, and if I go on and add other other words as "a man crossing the street," I am still only describing myself, what I am doing or thinking about. I am really saying nothing of the man whatever, I do not even affirm or imply that he exists ; but only that I am thinking as though he did. And yet that thinking might go on all the same if he does not, and even if I know that he does not.

Not so with perception, however. I perceive the table. There must be an object perceived, or there can be no act of perception. The verb is transitive, and requires for its completion an object acted upon, as truly as an agent acting. If I eat nothing I do not eat. If I perceive nothing I do not perceive. Now suppose there is no table, and no object whatever, then we replace the word "table" by the word "nothing" in the above proposition, and we have, "I perceive nothing." Hence, if I perceive nothing, I do not perceive, the act does take place, there is no act of perception, whatever else there may be.

Now, it seems to me, we have as clearly a case in which the principle of identity and contradiction is as applicable as it is to any of the synthetic propositions; or even to any of the mere self-evident axioms in mathematics. If the "table" be not a reality, the proposition becomes "I perceive nothing," and to perceive nothing is not to perceive—the act does not take place—the so-called act of perception is not an act of perception at all. Just as a so-called act of eating would not be an act of eating if there was nothing eaten.

Let us take another fundamental axiom in ontology, "Every effect has had a cause." I have spoken of this before, in making some remarks on the metaphysics of John Stuart Mill. I then called attention to the very significant fact that he replaces the word "effect" by the word "thing," and proceeds to discuss the axiom, as if it were "every thing must have had a cause." This substitution of one term for another is significant. It will hardly do to suppose that Mr. Mill consciously and intentionally played off a trick, or attempted to, on his readers. He was too shrewd, if not too candid a man for anything of that kind; and I certainly believe that he was too honest and candid to entertain, for one moment, the thought of such a thing. The only other hypothesis is, that with all his sagacity, and all the attention he had given to the doctrines he had undertaken to controvert, he had never really understood what he was attempting to refute.

It is not that "every *thing* has or has had a cause;" that is, every thing that we can imagine or conceive of or give a name to. I know of no way in which such a proposition can be proved. I do not know that such an attempt has ever been made by any one who has had much experience, or penetrated below the merest surface-thoughts in metaphysics. But the proposition "every *effect* has or has had a cause," is of a very different character. We speak of "effects" as things *produced* and not as mere objects—whether of perception, imagination or conception. The word "effect" implies more than the word "thing;" and it implies that we know more about an object than is implied when we call it merely a thing. It implies that we know that it has been *produced*. Otherwise we could not call it an effect; or in doing so we should be asserting of it what we do not know to be true.

With this explanation I think there will be no hesitation in admitting the truth of the axiom, and in admitting also, that its truth rests upon, and can be tested by the principle of identity and contradiction. If things are effects, they have been produced or caused, and if caused then they are effects and had a cause. Otherwise we have effects that are not effects—things produced that have not been produced.

But see the difference. An effect *ex vi termini* must have had a cause; and that cause was in existence *as an object* before it acted *as a cause*, or at least before the effect come into existence, if indeed, the effect be at all anything substantially and ontologically different from the cause itself. Hence a series; and a retrocession from any effect at present existing, to a cause, which is a First Cause, and not an effect at all, not caused by anything whatever, a substantial reality, an uncaused cause. And this is, at least, a *thing*, an objective substance, if not a Personal Cause or Creator.

If, therefore, we know anything *as an effect*, we know of it, that it had a cause. But it may be said this will not help us much. Perhaps not, this is only a matter of opinion and personal estimate. I do not know that it is very pertinent to the question before us. But it *does* help us to the conclusion that if there be any thing, fact or event, which *is* an effect, there was an object before it somewhere, and somewhen as a cause, which is not an effect but a cause, a cause only, a first cause, even the First Cause.

Nor does the extreme views of the Positivists help us much. They would deny causality altogether, discontinue the use of of the words "cause" and "law" as implying something that we know nothing about. They would substitute "sequence" and "order," for cause and law. Well: sequence implies one before the other, and when there is a series or sequence, there must have been one before which there was no "other"—a First One, therefore, call Him or it what we will. We *talk* of infinite series indeed, but they are infinite only in theory. Every series existing in fact had a first term, and has had a last one too, though that which is last to-day may not be so to-morrow.

But do you ask why not apply the rule to the First Cause also? I answer, because we know Him only as Cause. We know nothing of Him that implies that He is an effect. And besides; there must be somewhere an *un*caused Cause—a cause that existed before there was any effect. Otherwise there could have been no effect; and no such seqence or relation, would have been possible, or even conceivable. The very relation or conception, even, of cause and effect implies a first Cause or an uncaused Cause.

I do not propose in these Lectures to go into the detail of this method, or to explain, at length, how we are to reduce our propositions to a form that will exhibit their relation to this principle. I have done something towards it in the book already referred to. But I doubt if it is worth while to draw it out with as much of form and detail as has been done in the case of Arithmetic and Algebra. Here, as there, we must depend upon concurrent insight, and the assent which we can command by the exercise of it, as we go along. There can be no mere machine-logic in the case, no assent to conclusions, merely because certain approved formulæ have been used.

I will, however, give a few illustrations. Grammar and Logic sustain about the same relation to this higher method in Metaphysics as Arithmetic and Algebra do to the higher Mathematics. I will therefore give an illustration or two from each.

1. It is a law of Grammar that all verbs which are transitive in their active form or voice, take a passive form or voice. In this form the direct object of the active verb becomes the subject of the passive verb, as if "I *see* the table," "the table *is seen.*" I will give an application of this law bye-and-bye.

By another law of Grammar any noun following the preposition "of," may, with the preposition, be made into an adverb qualifying the verb, if the preposition is immediately preceded by one; or into an adjective qualifying the noun, if that be the word next before the preposition. Thus "ships of iron," are "iron ships." This is important in testing Sir William Hamilton's theory of perception. He holds that we are conscious of the perceived object, and that that object is some property, etc. Thus I am conscious of the whiteness of the paper. If so, "of whiteness," is either an adverb, denoting some quality of the act of consciousness; or an adjective qualifying the subject—the I. And in either case, what we regard as objective realities, are only subjective modes, or modes of modes, states and conditions of ourselves, as Berkeley and Hume, Fichte and Hegel have taught.

2. I give one or two examples from Logic. As the first, take the law that for any term or word used to denote an object the definition may be substituted. Thus, whenever we have the word triangle, we may replace it by the words "three-sided figure." Professor Tait for example, has just proposed to define force as the rate at which any thing moves. This may be a good *measure* of force, but replace the word "force" by this definition, wherever it occurs in his essay, and we shall see at once that the definition will not answer; we shall have a force that is not a force.

But the most comprehensive and the most important of all

changes are those that come from the application of Aristotle's dictum. From this it results that for any distributed term we may substitute a lower term, or qualify the one already in use by a modal, and for any undistributed term we may substitute a broader and more comprehensive one, or omit any modal or adjective that qualifies it.

Let us now recall an illustration which I have just used, and which I promised to take up again. "I see the table," therefore, the table is seen. Now "seen," being predicate in an affirmative proposition, is undistributed. It denotes also a mode in which the table is said to exist. But the summum genus includes all modes or forms of existence, and is irrespective of any. If now I take from the proposition "is seen," the word "seen," I enlarge the sphere of the predicate, as we have just seen we have a right to do; and as by taking it away, I leave no part of the predicate behind, I really substitute for it a symbol of the summum genus, and we have the "table is." That is, it exists as a substance, or a thing, in some mode, not now designated.

See now the importance of this. It follows that the *immediate* object of perception cannot be, as the philosophers have generally held, the *properties* of objects, or properties at all. For, suppose we have "I see redness," "redness" is a property. And we have "I see a property." But if "I see a property," "the property is seen," and if it is seen, it is, it exists as a something, is not a *property* of anything, it is a substance rather. Hence, if properties are perceived they are not properties, for whatever is perceived must be something, and not the mere property of anything, The moment we speak of them as properties, we pass them over into the category of substantial realities, that may be seen. What we call properties are not properties, if they are what we actually see in the acts of perception.

I have said that we can test the self-evident axioms by this principle. We can not *prove* them in the ordinary sense of the word, since for the most part, if not always, they have no middle term that can come, or be placed, between their subject and predicate. Hence, as I understand, the propriety of calling them *self*-evident; their truth is evident to insight without any process of deductive reasoning, without the intervention of any middle term.

In fact, all reasoning can be reduced to formulæ in which there are the two Premises, Major and Minor; and, unless one or both of them are conclusions of some previously formed syllogism, the Major Premise will be a *self*-evident axiom; and the Minor, either a definition, adopted *ex concessis*, or a proposition based on an act of perception, an elementary and simple observation of fact.

Hence we have clearly pointed out the two elements of knowledge; observation, including sense-perception and consciousness—the sensation and reflection of Locke—and self-evident axioms, based on insight, as I have explained it, and propose to call it. This takes the place of the ideas of Plato and Descartes; the schemata of Kant; the original suggestion of Brown, and the *a priori* ideas, or spontaneity of Cousin. It is an element which neither Locke, nor Hamilton, nor Mill recognized at all. And, of course, it is not recognized by Comte; nor is it recognized by any of the speculators in the physical sciences, whose theories we have been discussing, as Spencer, Huxley, etc., including all of those who think they can explain the phenomena of the physical Universe, without recognizing any thing more than matter, and the forces of matter.

And I think we have seen, that the principle of identity and contradiction, applies not only to the synthetical propositions in mathematics, but also, and fully as well, to certain primary truths in ontology, and in fact to all the fundamental axioms of the *a posteriori* sciences. In most cases it is not necessary to carry the reduction and transformation of the proposition until it *reaches* and is expressed in, the exact form A is A, or A is not A ; any more than mathematicians have found it necessary to follow out their demonstrations to their ultimate form and last statement. They usually stop and are satisfied when they come into full view of them, with clear insight and perfect certainty of the end. We may do the same; although, as I have insisted, we can in all cases, reduce the truth to the one form of expression ; or show the absurdity, if there be any, by the other. And in regard to absolute truth extending into the domain of philosophy, giving a foundation for ontology, that affirms the reality of external objects and gives a basis of absolute truth for all the physical sciences, the application is, I apprehend sufficiently manifest, even without the formal reduction of their statements to the principle we have been discussing. The principle is there, it extends its support to them all. It is enough if we can see it. The formal statement of it may be needed for theoretical or rhetorical purposes, but no such statement of it is necessary for any practical purposes whatever.

LECTURE VI.

REAL CAUSES.

The topic that remains for discussion is Real Causes. It seems to me to be preëminently *the* question of our age. As early as the thirteenth century, William of Occam, put in his caution against "multiplying entities, beyond any necessity for them," *non multiplicanda sunt entia præter necessitatem.* And four centuries later, the great Newton, found the same necessity for protesting against the multiplication of unreal causes. The one was a metaphysician and aimed to restrict the pretensions of knowledge to realities. The other was a physicist—the greatest name, perhaps, in the whole history of the physical sciences. And he found it necessary, in the interest of science to put men on their guard against referring to, as agents and causes of observed phenomena in nature, what were no real cause, but only the *entia præter necessitatem*, of the great Mediæval Nominalist. And now, as then, we find men who are inclined to trust in these unrealities, until they will not believe in either a soul within them, or a God above them.

I think it will be better, before proceeding with the main subject of this Lecture, to devote a few moments to the consideration of another matter of great practical importance in its bearing on the main subject now before us. I refer to the law of coördination in cognition. We have had our attention already called to this principle, as that on which Herbert Spencer has taken issue with Sir William Hamilton, asserting as Hamilton had not done, the existence and reality of what Spencer calls the Noumenon—and Hamilton had been content to regard and call the Unknowable.

Of the reality of such a principle or law of intelligence, there can be no doubt. The only question is as to its nature and the extent of its application.

We shall perhaps put ourselves in the best position for understanding it and appreciating its nature and applications if we begin with certain *a posteriori* manifestations of it.

It has long been well known that the deaf have no "idea" of sound, and that the blind have no "idea" of light or of color. And with them, imagination is also limited accordingly. They can not even *imagine*, the one of them how an object *looks*, nor the other what *sound* or *noise* it makes. All the sensible properties derived or derivable, from these senses are excluded for them from the domain of knowledge. They may indeed, use the words and terms that are common in the vocabularies of those that can see and hear. But they attach no meaning to them, or, at least, a very grotesque one ; as when the blind boy said he knew what the color red was, it was like the sound of a drum.

But it has not been so generally considered that these unfortunates are just as deficient in the "ideas" of *darkness* and of *silence*. The blind man can attach no more meaning to the word darkness, than he can to those which denote light and the various colors of the objects we see. The deaf man has no more idea of silence than he has of sound, although he is immersed in silence all the while, and that is the only thing in that line of which he has ever had any experience.

In the cases cited the coördination may be regarded as between two successive stages of the same object. But in some cases as we shall soon see, there must be two objects existing and cognized at the same instant. But it is rather a nice point, perhaps, to determine precisely the limit to the powers of imagination in this respect. Although I do not think that one who had never seen a black object or a white one, could imagine an object of either of these colors, or these no-colors, as we may happen to regard them, I am, nevertheless, inclined to think that having seen objects of both of those colors, he could imagine one of a color that is a mixture of the two, some shade of gray, for instance. So too, I think with the sight of red and blue, we could imagine violet; with red and yellow he could imagine orange, and with yellow and blue, green, etc.

If now we generalize this, we come to the conclusion, that we can not imagine any *original* element of knowledge, though we can in imagination combine and compound any and all of those that we have, possibly without limit. In this way we can imagine objects of forms, sizes, proportions and combinations of parts, such as have never been seen and have never existed. And so, too, we can ascribe, in imagination, to objects real or imagined, properties, which they have not, and never had, and which, perhaps, they could not have. And finally, we can combine in imagination, as we can in fact by mixing the pigments, such properties as we have, to make new varieties and shades. These, however, will be mixtures and combinations of the simple and unresolvable properties. But of the simple and unresolvable elements, we cannot imagine any one, nor in any way, or by any mental process, have a thought of it.

Looking at all the adjectives we have, we see at once, that

they all, and in all departments of knowledge, admit of being resolved into the two classes, already indicated, the one denoting what we call simple and elementary properties, such as the colors, red, blue, etc, and the other denoting those which are composite. Or, *perhaps*, we may have another class, which are not objective at all, but only inferential. Thus, I think, that extension is unquestionably a simple property, such as could not be imagined by one who had not cognized, by either sight or touch, an extended object. But I think also that one who had seen an extended object, could and would, by either insight or imagination, think of its divisibility, and perhaps he could imagine it as being divided, without ever having seen such an operation ; simply because by his insight into the nature of objects as extended, he knows that they are all, and of necessity, divisible. Extension and divisibility are both of them simple and elementary properties ; they can neither of them be resolved into others as we resolve orange into red and yellow, gray into black and white, etc. Extension is objective and given in sense-perception. But divisibility may, as I am inclined to think, be a result of either a perception of the act of division, or of an insight into the nature of extended objects.

And here I think we have the limit. Every property which we ascribe to any object *that is not resolvable into two or more simpler and elementary properties, must have been derived by some act of cognition.* No such property can have been the result of any act of mere imagination ; and *all others may have been* originated in imagination or fancy.

This doctrine of coördination in cognition, will doubtless need to be very carefully considered and cautiously guarded before it can be safely put to practical use in determining the extent and limit within which we are to believe in real cause.

It lies at the very foundation; and can hardly be called into use except for the purpose of determining a very few fundamental facts, such as are of the most elementary character.

I think that we could not perceive by the *eyes* at all, if there were not more than one object in the field of vision *at the same time*, or at least two parts of the same object so diverse in color or shade as to appear to the eye different in this respect.

It must also be carefully noted that I am speaking of the *original act* of cognition, rather than any subsequent act of *re*-cognition. If one has *ever* seen a red object, he can ever afterward imagine any object to be red*, whether it be so or not. So, too, he can have false perception, supposing that he sees objects, that are red when they are of some other color, or possibly there is no object at all. But without having once *seen* a red object it never happens even in the wildness of our wildest dreams, or in the madness of delirium that we transcend this law.

And I think also, that we can go one step farther. I assume at present, the objective reality of material things; and I assume that they produce in us the sensations by which we perceive them. I know, of course, that there are those who doubt this doctrine. I will attend to their view, in another connection. And I think I shall be able to effectually dispose of it when we come to it.

Assuming then that objects are external, and that they produce in us the sensations we preceive them by; these objects, any two of them that are seen at any one time, must belong to

---

*Of course, I am aware of the fact, that even the power to imagine objects by their colors, gradually disappears, in most cases, from those who become blind. But the fact is of no importance to the subject before us now.

a common proximate genus, that is, they must have essentia common to them both. If, for example, they are seen by the eye, they must belong to the proximate genus, one of whose essentia is visibility. Then, they must *differ* in color; and color becomes the differentia of the two coördinated objects. Now we say that we see them, as two and discriminate them by their color. But the phrase "by their color," denotes a cause or instrument—which, in the nature of the case, must have existed in the order of time, before the act of discrimination could have taken place. We have then, in the sentence, "I distinguish them *by their colors,*" three elements, (1) "*we*" the agent, or the efficient cause, (2) "*colors*" the instrumental cause, and (3) *the act of distinguishing* or discriminating—which is a result or an effect of the two causes. This act requires the *combined* action of the two causes, and of course, therefore, it implies their reality and existence, before the act could have taken place, so that without each and both of them the act of perception could never have occurred at all. Hence the color could not have been created in or by the act; for it was necessary as a cause or instrument to the very existence or performance of the act.

I am aware that those who have followed me in my remarks on the use of language, may object that I have been speaking of *color* all along, as though it were an objective reality, a thing that could be seen—as being in fact a real cause. So I have: but then, it must be remembered, that we often find it convenient to continue to use terms and forms of expression that grew out of an abandoned theory, long after we have ceased to hold the theory. We continue to speak of sunrise, as though we believed in the old ante-Copernican theory of the cosmical motions. The only limit to the continued use of such "*survivals,*" is, that everybody shall understand them;

and no body so use them as to mislead others, or necessarily imply the old theory. And I think I have complied with these conditions in this case. If we will replace the terms "color," etc., by its proper logical equivalent, "colored object," we shall find that the propositions are none the less intelligible and consecutive on that account, although they will doubtless be found to be much less acceptable to the accomplished rhetorician.

And I do not see but that these remarks, and this line of reasoning applies as well to acts of insight, as to acts of sight, or to any other means than the eye. We cannot *see* whether by sight, or by insight, what is not, and does not exist to be seen.

This law of coördination, it must be remembered, relates only to the beginning of knowledge, and so, of course, only to finite minds. It does not pertain to its retention or permanence. The blind that have once seen retain their ideas of color a long time after total blindness. But if there be an Intelligent Being, who has no beginning the law does not apply to Him.

But it is time, and more than time, to come to the more immediate object of this Lecture, "real causes."

It is manifest that that cannot be a real cause, which is not itself real. The word "thing" is more comprehensive than "cause," just as man is more comphehensive than "Englishman," quadruped, than horse. An object may be a thing—an object and not be a cause—or at least we can so think of it as a thing—a substance. Or to apply a rule referred to in the last Lecture, we have "AB is a cause." But if AB is a cause, it must be, and be something, a substantial something, in order to be a cause. Causality or causation is but a mode in which things may exist. And they may also exist in other modes or at least out of that mode in some other; although they can not exist except in some mode. If we say of anything "it is a cause," we may drop the word "cause" from the predicate; and then we merely affirm that it is, it exists, is something. To this there can be no *real* exception. There are only two apparent exceptions.

The first is the case in which the predicate is a negative term, or one with no intensity, as the logicians say—thus, "It is nothing." This is really a negative proposition and hence does not come under the rule at all. But if we say "this is space," "this is substance," etc., as the predicate does not denote any object by its properties, or as existing in any mode, the rule does not apply, and such cases constitute an apparent, but not a real exception, to the rule.

The other case is that in which the predicate is an abstract term, whether used in the singular or in the plural number. As if we say "red is a color," "hardness is a property," or "ductility and fusibility are properties of iron." These expressions are apparent exceptions, indeed. But they are not strictly true, although in general and accredited use. In strictness of speech all we can say in such cases is, that "red is *the name* of a color," etc. We are really speaking only of the word "red," and are giving to it a verbal definition. We are not speaking of the thing at all.

Of abstract terms we can only give verbal definitions except when we use them by metonymy.

But to our tests. In the first place we may have a test from the laws of language I have already described, which will show what we have no right *at present* to regard as real causes.

We have no right to regard as a real cause, anything which we cannot denote by a concrete term, nothing in fact, which we denote by either, (1) an abstract term, or, (2) a negative term, or, (3) by a mere etymological compound. None of these terms denote objects by what they are, or by what they are known to do, or to be.

It is easy to apply this rule, and to test it also. Suppose I say, "matter is extended." Is the word matter abstract, concrete, or negative? If I put it into its adjective form and then put after it the most comprehensive concrete term that we know of—the word thing—and say, "*material things* are expanded," we see at once, that the proposition means the same as before. "Material things" are what we mean by the term matter. If we say "the mind thinks" and then put the expression "a mental thing thinks," we have the same thought expressed in another and less elegant form; "mental thing" is just what we mean by the word "*mind*."

But suppose we take another example and say "heat expands all things." Is heat concrete and abstract? Is it a real cause or only an objectified abstraction? Try it and see; "heated bodies expand others." This is true, and is, I suppose what we meant to say by the use of the former expression. At any rate it is all that we know to be true, and all, therefore, that we have any right to affirm. But by "heated bodies" we certainly do not mean the same as by the word "heat." Bodies are things in themselves; heat is but a mode, condition or property of a thing.

Now this method is perfectly good as far as it goes; and it goes to this extent. Replace the noun by its adjective, and place after it the name "thing," and if we make thereby no change in our meaning, the word must be regarded, at present, as concrete; and the thing denoted by it must be considered a real cause. But if it changes the meaning, so that the proposition in one form is one thing, and something else in the other, if it appears, in fact, to be speaking of one subject in one form, and of another in the other, the term is abstract, and does not denote what we actually regard as a real cause.

Hence the general proposition that whatever we denote by concrete terms are, at present, and in our present state of knowledge must be regarded by the common sense of mankind, and to a considerable extent by the fundamental conditions of thought, as real causes. And whatever is denoted by either as an abstract or a negative term, is not so.

But this rule or test alone is not sufficient. We want something that goes deeper into the subject than mere words.

I suggest the following tests, as in my opinion, final and complete.

1. In the first place, sense-perception is a test, and gives us knowledge of true entities—real substances.

Whatever we perceive must be real—a real object, or it could not be perceived. I think I have already sufficiently disposed of the theories of those who hold that what we call objects are but modes of ourselves; and of the theories also which teach that what we perceive is only the properties of objects. On the first hypothesis, perception could not take place. To perceive nothing, is not to perceive. And on the other, what we call properties, are made, for the occasion, at least, substances and real properties. To be seen, they must be—be something, and not the mere properties of things.

They must be causes also: for perception, as contra-distinguished from imagination, implies sensation, and is conditioned by it. And in producing the sensations by which we perceive them, objects act as causes, upon our organs of sense.

2. As a second rule or test, we have the following. We are

able to prove by insight into certain processes, the reality of a cause or an agent, even when the cause or agent may not be actually seen, and possibly cannot for one reason or another, ever become an object of immediate cognition.

We have examples in the material world. The case most commonly cited is that of the discovery of the planet Neptune. An astronomer had observed a perturbation in the motions of Uranus, and believing that there was a cause outside of the planet itself, he computed the indications which the perturbance gave; and on pointing the telescope to the place where the cause had been indicated, Neptune was found. To-day also, there are phenomena which prove the existence of planetary masses inside the orbit of Mercury, and so near the sun that they have not been seen, and probably never can be seen by any one on this earth.

But perhaps the chief value of this mode of proof depends upon its enabling us to prove realities that have no sensible properties.

Turning to consciousness: that is, a process of interior observation. It is expressed by a passive, or at least by an intransitive verb. We say "I am conscious." But we cannot put any direct object, as the grammarians call it, after the word "conscious." It must be followed by the preposition "of,' "conscious of." And the word that follows the preposition' "of" is always the name of some mental act or state, as perceiving, remembering, willing, etc. Even Sir William Hamilton in his unreserved devotion to his theory of cognition, never ventured upon a solecism so absurd as that. He would say "I am conscious of the table," which is certainly unusual, harsh and contrary to fundamental laws. But he never ventured to say, "I am conscious the table," as we do say, "I perceive the table." I should regard this fact alone, as a sufficient refutation of Sir William's theory on this subject.

If we say, "I am conscious of perceiving," the limitation or modal "perceiving," makes the expression equivalent to "I am perceiving-conscious"—or, "I-perceiving am conscious."

But by our insight into the nature of the process—perceiving, imagining, etc., we see that it is a *process*—a mere *mode* of existence, and a process or mode only, not at all a substantial thing; no real entity. There must, therefore, be something that perceives, imagines, etc., or there can be no perception or imagination. Otherwise a mode is not a mode, and a process is a substance that proceeds, and not a mere process. Hence, the mind must be a real cause, in accordance with the opinion of all unsophisticated people, and in accordance also with the usage of all languages.

It has been suggested that the phenomena of dreams first led men to think of a soul or spirit within them as something distinct from the body. It is hardly possible that such experience should not suggest the doctrine of a soul, at an early period of human history, even if there had been nothing before to lead their thoughts in that direction. On awaking from sleep the dreamer would be perfectly sure that his body had remained where it was when he went to sleep, and yet he would remember that he had been in other places, and seen persons that could not have been near his body, any more than his body could have gone to them. Nothing more natural therefore, than the thought that there is a soul—a self—a something within the body, which is not only unlike it, but which can leave the body and exist in the exercise of conscious thought and volition while the body lies insensible to all around, in profound sleep.

But a more careful analysis leads me to doubt whether without something previous to such experience, the doctrine of a soul as distinct from the body, would have arisen. Although there can be no doubt that the experience both of dreams, and of swooning or syncope, would do much to strengthen the belief in the reality of a soul, and to modify the doctrine held and taught concerning it, another method, it seems to me, would more certainly lead men to think of the me--the *ego*—the self, as something distinct from all its surroundings, including even the body itself. The first effort to do a thing that we cannot do, would suggest the idea of two antagonistic somethings, the one striving and trying, and the other counteracting and resisting. If I but try to lift a weight that I cannot raise from the ground I become well aware that there are at least *two* objects in the Universe, and that myself is one of them and only one. Or, again, if there is a pain in my finger, I become conscious of both it and myself—the *finger aches* indeed, but it is *I myself that feel* the pain. I feel it and not another; it is myself and nobody else.

But how about the perceived object? I have expressly reserved this question for consideration in this place.

We have already seen that if there is any act of perception there must be a perceived object, which is a real entity, and not a mere property of an object.

But is there an act of perception at all?

Of course, it will not be quite satisfactory to anybody who proposes the question, merely to say, that we are conscious of perceiving; for they do not deny this. They say we mistake our opinion of the fact, for the fact itself. We are conscious, and we *judge* the act to be perception.

I waive the question whether in this case the distinction is well taken ; I think in fact that it is not. But conceding that it is, I fall back on the law of coördination.

Perception as a mental act or state, has a differentia of its own that distinguishes it from imagination, memory, etc., just as red has a differentia that distinguishes it from white or blue, etc. And as the man, who, although possessed of the sense of sight to its fullest extent, had never seen an object that is red, could have no "idea" of such objects, could attach no meaning whatever to the name denoting the color , nay, more, if all men were and had always been like him in this respect, there would be no names anywhere for such a color ; so, precisely so, if there were no acts of perception distinct from imagination, etc., and having that peculiar and special differentia of perception, on account of which, we infer the existence of the perceived object—we should have no name for the act of perception, no conception of it ; and even the *question* whether external objects exist or not, could never had occurred to man —not even to philosophers in the profoundest or in the wildest of their imaginings.

And this for the general proposition that external objects exist as we see them, and as the common sense of mankind has always believed them to exist. But this conclusion does not extend to any one particular object. There is always the possibility of false perception, by which we think we see an object when there is no object to be seen. Hence the assertion of the existence of any particular object is only a probable proposition—the probabilities amounting in most cases to a practical, or as we say, a moral certainty, sufficient for all the practical purposes of life. But unless there were something in existence after the manner in which we suppose external objects to exist, and unless we had actually perceived some one or more of them, there could be no belief in their existence—no thought of them and no question about the existence of any one of them at all.

What we thus cognize or prove to exist must not only be *real as entities*—but *adequate as causes*, also. To be causes they must be, as entities; and to produce their effects they must be adequate to their production. Hence a knowledge of the effects is an essential part of the argument. If I see a piece of white paper, I know that the object is capable of affecting the retina of my eye, or I could not see it as an object at all. And it must affect it in one certain way and not in any other, or I should not see it as *white*.

So when Le Verrier predicted a planet from the perturbations in the movements of Uranus, he assumed that Uranus was mere matter, inert like all other mere inorganic masses and so incapable of *voluntary* motion. He did not suppose that it wandered out of its path spontaneously or of its own free will, and so he inferred the existence of another planet. He might have supposed that there was some *person* that turned it aside. He might have referred the phenomena to the immediate act of God. But he observed the law that precludes us from ascribing to the causes which we discover anything more than is necessary to make them adequate to the observed effect.

I have said a good deal about intelligence and voluntary action in dumb animals. The subject is worth alluding to here, for more purposes than one. So long as we knew nothing of reflex action—its nature and extent—there seemed to be no adequate cause of the actions of animals, except mind or soul within them, as there is in man. But the discoveries made in that line have entirely changed the ground of the argument. We see now that the nervous system considered as a piece of mere material mechanism is adequate to all that animals do; and hence the inference that they have mind and volition is creating a cause *prœter necessitatem,* altogether beyond the necessities of the case.

Here then we must stop. Observation and Demonstration are our two, and our only methods of proving or verifying the existence of realities and real causes.

Observation is two-fold. Sense-perception for objects in the outward world—the not-me—and Consciousness for the phenomena within—the me.

Demonstration by means of insight *from observed facts.* The limitation is important, for Demonstration in Ontology differs from the process we call by that name in Mathematics; not at all, perhaps, in the process itself; but widely in the starting point. In Mathematics we begin with a hypothesis or a definition and end in the establishment of a law or a condition of existence. But in Ontology we begin with an observed fact. First of all, the observed fact of consciousness. From this we prove the reality of the subject and the object—the perceiving *ego,* and the perceived entity. And from either, as objects, we may proceed to prove other objects, as well as truths and laws concerning objects, which are based—not as in mathematics, on the mere possibility of their existence, without regard to their properties—but *upon* their properties—treating them as individuals, in classes, species and genera.

But we must stop here. The mere process of abstraction creates nothing; it produces no reality. The object with which we begin is a reality. This paper is white—the object is a reality—but "its whiteness" is not, though the paper is *really* white. The *whiteness* is neither substance, nor cause, nor yet object. It is a convenient fiction and nothing more.

I do not think that the reverse of the argument from cause to effect, although of inestimable value elsewhere, is of any importance, in this relation. Doubtless, if we could ever know that a Being was in the act of creation, in the sense of making something out of nothing, we should know from that act, that something was being created, and would exist thereafter as a real entity. But in practical affairs, if we know, for example, that the two gases—hydrogen and oxygen—are combining, we merely know that two substances—entities—are about to exist in another form ; but no new entity or substance can be produced by that process, or by any other process that man can institute.

Nor yet can hypothesis create anything. We can suppose or assume the existence of entities at will, and without limit. And the process may be useful for certain purposes. But if in doing so we create phenomena to be explained, or imagine unreal causes to explain them, our theories will break down and fail us if we go one step beyond the real entities and substantial causes already existing in nature.

The two classes of objects which chiefly occur to us are "*ideas*" and "*forces*."

No one is conscious of ideas. The assumption or hypothesis that there are such entities, was found convenient by Plato, and has been continued in one form or another to our day. Cousin assumes their reality, as *entities in the mind*, as the basis of his Philosophy, and of his argument against Locke. And yet he says in that very course of lectures, (*Lecture X, second series,*) "*there is nothing real but things, and the mind with its operations, that is, its judgments.*" Whatever liberty of construction we may give to the words "its operations," we certainly must exclude ideas from their scope. And yet Cousin not only speaks of our having ideas, but of our being conscious of them and of their being immediate objects of consciousness. Certainly such expressions are not well considered. Nobody is conscious of *having the idea* of space, for example. He is conscious only of *thinking of* space, conscious as Cousin says, "of the mind and its operations," when thinking of it. Ideas then, may be a convenient hypothesis, but they are no substantial entities, no real causes.

And so with "forces." If we speak of real things as "forces," as wind, water, steam, etc., there can be no objection to the use of the word—for they are real entities. But when we speak of light, and heat, and gravity, etc., as real forces, we are transcending the limits of known reality. The words as derived from adjectives and verbs by abstraction. We know of no light as distinct from a luminous body, of no heat as distinct from a heated substance, of no gravity when there is no gravitating mass.

The claim is sometimes put forth that we have a right to regard certain objects as realities, on account of the use we can make of them as means of explaining phenomena that we certainly do observe. Nay, it is said that we cannot understand certain phenomena, as the transmission of light and heat, without them. Well, this fact may demonstrate our infirmity; it can hardly prove their existence as substantial entities. When such statements are made I cannot help thinking that we had better stop and consider whether we have not already committed one error in supposing light and heat to be entities that need transmission, or that can be transmitted at all.

One of our leading scientific men says, "In this long history of animal life, I have said nothing of what Life itself really is, . . . because I know nothing." But he has *done* something, though he does does not appear to know it. He has *made* it an entity—a real cause. No wonder, therefore, that *as a real entity* he knows nothing about it, for as such it is nothing ; it is only a mode, and as a mode of existence, or of an entity it is as intelligible and as well comprehended perhaps, as any other mode. As an entity—a real cause—it is nothing and of nothing—nothing is all that can be said.

And thus I differ from the Realists so-called, in not ascribing reality to abstractions, and from the Nominalists in recognizing the mind as a real cause ; and, as implied in the observed phenomena of both mind and matter, as we shall see more fully bye-and-bye, the existence of a Supreme Being, who is real without being material, and substantial without being extended.

What we shall ascribe to mind will vary with the progress of knowledge. It is vastly less now than it was before the discovery of the nature of reflex action. But it may be, and I think it most likely that it will be, much more hereafter than it is now.

But of one thing we may be certain. Men who have well considered the subject—men who are entitled either to have, or to express, any opinion on the subject—will consider the mind as a concrete reality—a substantial thing a *vera causa*. No one will define it as only "the series of his own states of consciousness." No one will speak of it as only "a phase of nature's order," or as "a force produced by nervous action." I think no definition better than Hamilton's is likely to be found, "Mind is to be understood as the subject of the various "internal phenomena of which we are conscious—or that sub-"ject of which consciousness is the general phenomenon"—or manifestation rather, "Mind can be defined only from [by] "its manifestations," we can describe it only as an agent—by that which it does, and not at all as an object or by what it is.

I am inclined to think, however, that it will be regarded as the *immediate* object of consciousness—though I have not so treated it in these Lectures. If so, the expression "I am conscious of perceiving," will be regarded as equivalent to "I am conscious of self-perceiving—or perceiving-self." And the preposition "of," will take after it, a concrete term.

I do not intend to discuss here what is sometimes called the *autonomy* of the brain and nerve cells. A nerve cell as soon as it begins to exist is a *living* structure ; and in all living structures, *as long as they live,* there are chemical changes going on. I do not deny—on the contrary, it seems to me likely, not to say certain—that these changes which are thus going on, may occasion acts that are precisely like reflex action in their character, though not really so in their origin. This kind of *autonomous* activity, may constitute a large part of the active life of men and animals. And it is in fact often spoken of and called *spontaneous* activity. It is indeed, the "spontaneity" that we find in nature, and the only form of spontaneity we find there. But it is after all subject to physical laws—such as we see everywhere in chemical action. It is not the spontaneity that we become conscious of in ourselves.

The history of the origin and development of these two coördinate ideas, the ideas of spontaneity and inertia, is interesting and instructive in more ways than one.

From the earliest stages of human life, men were conscious of spontaneous activity in themselves and their own actions. Naturally they ascribed this kind of activity to all things else. We see the effect of this alike in the pantheism of the early Hindoo nations and in the fetichism of all the Mongol and

Negro races, and the tendency to it among those who are lowest in intellectual culture, everywhere. Without this fact the religious history of man is incomprehensible and inexplicable. The same tendency to ascribe spontaneity to all things around us, still remains as the chief support, in my estimation, of the common belief in the voluntariness of the actions of dumb animals.

Its recognition among the students of physical science was as we have seen abundantly in the course of these Lectures, the chief obstacle to the progress of those sciences, all through the Greek period as well as during the Middle Ages. Their division of motions into the two classes, "natural" or those that are in a straight line, and those that are contrary to nature or not in a straight line, implies the admission, though not the consciously adopted belief, that those bodies that moved in curved lines had some *voluntary* power of changing and directing their movements in their own way. Hence, by the admission of an unreal cause they failed to find the real nature of curvilinear motion.

And the doctrine of the inertia of all mere matter was not fully realized until the time and labors of Newton. I do not find the word "*inertia*" in use in this sense before the time of Kepler. And he is said to have been the first to use it at all. The doctrine was not recognized in chemistry until a still later period. And until this fact of the inertia of all matter was distinctly recognized and made the basis and actual cornerstone of all Physical Sciences, no one of them was placed on its proper foundation, or could make satisfactory progress.

But there must be the two, inert matter and spontaneously-acting agents, especially the latter, actually existing somewhere ; or we should have had no such word, no such conception ; any more than in a world where all the people are blind and have always been so, there could be words denoting light and darkness and the various colors which distinguish the objects we see around us.

And again, as already intimated in these Lectures, I think that the fact of motion and change in nature implies a Beginning—or, perhaps I had better say a Beginner—who is not material. Each change is an effect; and its immediate cause was also an effect of something before it. And thus we have a series running back indefinitely. But a series without a first term is an impossibility. And, moreover, the first term is never produced as the succeeding terms are, or in accordance with the law of the series. It must have had a cause and a law of its own, and peculiar to itself. Otherwise it would not have been the first term at all.

I see not how we can escape the necessity of admitting the existence of a Supreme Being somewhere. If, as we have just said, this series of phenomena in nature had a beginning, there must have been a Supreme Being, a First Cause to cause it to begin.

But on the supposition that it had no beginning it is eternal. And with time enough, all things that are *possible*—the bad and the worst, as well as the good and the best, must become *real* also; unless there is a Supreme Being, a Sovereign Ruler to prevent it. And must not an Infinite Being, if he did not exist at first, be among the things already produced? Surely such a Being is conceivable, and therefore possible. It will not do to say "*not yet*"; for eternity is long enough for all things that are in themselves possible. There must have been time enough for all things whose existence does not imply a contradiction in terms, many times over—in fact, any number of times, already. If, therefore, there was no God at first, as a Creator and Lawgiver, there must have been one *produced* by this very process of evolution and development long ago, as a necessary result. I see no way of escaping this conclusion.

And miracles too ; for aught I can see. If there was before all else an Infinite Being, who created this world and gave it its law—even though that law were the law of evolution—the very act of creating, of originating and starting it off, must have been miraculous, in the only proper sense we can attach to the word. And whether He has interposed *miraculously*, or by way of miracle since, is merely a question of history. The supposition is possible, and perhaps, on the whole rather probable.

But if there were no such Being at the beginning as creator and cause, then as we have just seen the very process of evolution and development must have produced one. And I think that in the nature of the case there can be but One Supreme or Infinite Being. Spinoza has proved that. But He must be a miracle-worker, else He is not infinite ; He lacks one attribute, the possession of which would add to His being, and a miracle-worker would be greater than He. The very conception of such a Being implies superiority to nature, and power over it. He that *did* originate laws can suspend them ; He that ordained gravity as the law of masses, can also, upon occasion, ordain that gravity shall not act so as to draw down too roughly, the sparrow that flutters and falls. He that gave life and raised the unliving atoms to be a vital frame can certainly control that life, so as to suspend and restore it at pleasure. He that is above all things, surely for Him there is nothing that He can not do. The only limit to His power is nonentity. He can not do that which is nothing when it is done ; as, to make *two* hills without a valley between them, or a crooked line that is shorter than a straight one between the same points. Or is there no such Being? Why not? If this evolution has been going on infinitely—if it had no beginning, and its tendency is, as all admit and claim that it is, and has been for countless millions of years, *upwards*, it must have produced such an Infinite Being an infinite time ago. And that, as it seems to me is about the same as "*In the Beginning.*"

The recognition of this First Cause may be no necessity for any branch of the Natural or mere Physical, Sciences. They deal with second causes and intermediate stages and terms in this, only not endlessly, long series. For the man of this nineteenth century who would write a history of Greece, it is no matter whether the earth had a beginning to its existence or not, or whether man has been living on its surface ten millions, ten, or only six thousand years. In either case the period of which he would write, and the events he would describe, are too far from the beginning, to be influenced by any diversity of views that may be held concerning it.

So with Natural Science. The very idea of cause, and the relation of cause and effect implies, indeed, a First Cause. But then, we are so far from that first act of causation, that no special influence can come from it upon the observations and conclusions of to-day; if we confine ourselves to the appropriate sphere of science. But it is narrow-minded and unphilosophical to hold, that because we have nowhere encountered any First Cause, or any act of primary causation there can have been none. Many things must have happened on this earth, the likes of which *we* have never seen. The Universe certainly has not always gone on as it is going now. At all events it did not begin as it is now going. At the starting off there was something unusual, a different order and another

Cause besides those that the Physicist now finds in his manipulations.

Nor will the hypothesis of alternating extremes—maxima and minima of heat and cold, expansion and condensation, help us much. They are mere "*dead points,*" where the Universe comes to periods of "complete equilibrium or rest" as Herbert Spencer calls them. For we must remember that we are speaking of the Universe, the sum total of all things that exist. And when *it* comes to "equilibrium" or "rest," all its parts and particles are inactive, and there can be no outside mass of matter to act upon it, and set it in motion again. Its own particles and parts have ceased to act on each other. There is nothing to carry it through the maximum or the minimum, where from condensation it should begin to expand, or from expansion it should begin to condense. There must, therefore, be a Personal Agent somewhere outside of it—or in it—to carry it through these points, or it would have remained in the first one it reached, forever. And, of course, if the Universe is eternal, such an one must have been reached long ago; so long that nobody can tell how long.

A cause there must be, then, and a First Cause. And He must be not only real but adequate also. We cannot resolve His nature into ideas, with Plato and the pantheists; for then He would not be real. Nor yet can we resolve it into mere abstractions and laws, with the materialists; for then He would not be adequate. He must be intelligent or there would be no order or comprehensibility in the Universe. He must be capable of volition and purpose; for before He acted there was nothing to act on Him as motive or cause. And these—intelligence and power of choice—constitute Pensonality.

Many object to ascribing personality to God, because as they think, it implies limitation, localization, restraint, and perhaps caprice and mere arbitrary rule. But all these are the mere accidents of personality, as we see it manifested in our fellow-men. Perhaps they are, all of them, inseperable from finite personality anywhere. But they are no attributes of an infinite Person. Infinity, from its very nature transcends all these conditions and limitations. We may not be able to comprehend it—we certainly cannot imagine it. And all our conceptions of it, do the best we can, are undoubtedly inadequate and to some extent anthropomorphitic—but some conception of it, more or less adequate or inadequate we all have.

And He must be a Lawgiver also. It is true that facts, in nature, suggest a law ; and, by induction we find that law. But, *in all contingent matter*, law is only the realization of the will and purpose of some person, one who chose to have things as they are, but might have chosen to have them otherwise ; and His choice would have made them so. In necessary matter this personal influence not only does not appear, —it is precluded. But in all the inductive Sciences, what the scientist finds, and all he can find, is an expression of the will of a Personal Lawgiver.

To the views thus presented, few, if any, I apprehend, will object. Men object only when when we begin to talk of a God Who can lay His commands on us—command us to do things and punish us if we do them not. Here is the practical difficulty, the grand sticking point, the insuperable obstacle at which most unbelievers hesitate. But I do not appreciate the force of the objection. It is certain that man often needs, for his own good, to conform to laws, the reasons of which he cannot see until after he is either enjoying the fruits of obedience, or suffering the enduring consequences of his mistakes. Restraint is better than the freedom that allows us to do wrong.

Upon the natural order, there is certainly based a supernatural. In the lower order—the order of Nature—the consequences of any violation of law follow surely and inevitably, whether we know the law or not ; the burnt finger smarts none the less, whether we did or did not know that fire will burn. But in the higher order—the Supernatural—no man feels shame, remorse, or regret even, unless he *knows* that the act he has done is wrong. Into this higher order we rise the moment we become capable of thought and voluntary action. Here we enter upon a new state of discipline. We not only become capable of knowing and comprehending higher laws, which have no application or force below us, but we become responsible also for the knowledge and observance of them. The worst of the pains, as well as the most cherished and characteristic enjoyments of our lives in this world, and all our hopes of a life hereafter, depend on the laws and conditions of that sphere. They are found nowhere, not even the germ or prophecy of them, in mere inorganic matter. They do not enter into plant life. The dumb animals know nothing of them. From man they extend upwards, and reach a limit we know nothing of. God is above them, and "over all, blessed forever."

But none of the methods we have considered include among the real entities, either the "ideas" and "faculties" of which the psychologists have said so much, nor yet the "forces" of which the physical philosophers make so much account at the present day. Their effects are never seen except in the presence of real causes, which are known to be indisputably such, and which are sufficient to account for all the effects we see. Hence, we must, at present, regard the hypothesis that assumes that they are real causes or entities at all, as wholly gratuitous and unwarranted by any principle of a sound philosophy.

No immediate change in the use of language is, however, to be expected. Perhaps it is not to be desired. So long as physicists use these abstract terms, as mere convenient metonymies—the fact that they are so used being well understood and admitted by all, no harm can come of the use; and much is gained by way of brevity and comprehensiveness of expression.

It may be, as already said, and for the reasons given, that mere science has no need to take into account either a First Cause, or the final causes of things. But *Philosophy* must take account of both. Science has no authority to deny, and no justification for denying their reality. Whatever is possible may be real. Only Omniscience can affirm a universal negative in contingent matter. No finite mind can affirm that there is not an Infinite Mind somewhere. Hardly can we say that He is not at work in the phenomena around us, even those with which we are most familiar and think we know the best—in the gravitation, in the attraction and repulsion, the analysis and synthesis, the successions and changes that make up the sum of nature's phenomena.

Even while these pages are going through the press, one of the foremost scientific men of our country says, "Light, Heat, "Electricity and Magnetism, Chemical Affinity and Motion, "are now considered different forms of the same Force; and "the opinion is rapidly gaining ground that Life, or Vital "Force, is only another phase of the same power." If by "light" he means anything else than "luminous bodies," and by "heat" anything but heated masses or molecules of matter, and by "life" anything besides living tissues and cells, what he calls Force or Power can be nothing but God Himself, at work in those phenomena.

I am well aware that the ignorant and superstitious are always looking for "miracles" and "interpositions" in their behalf. And the whole history of science is an illustration of the fact that scientific discovery is constantly relegating what has been regarded as "miracle," to "the order and course of nature," until scientific men have come to accept it as an axiom, that there are no miracles now. It is well; for it teaches us to trust to ourselves and to the laws of nature as being the chief factor of that providence by which God governs the world. But we cannot, and we *do* not forgo all trust or faith in Providence. In the lowest and most ignorant it may take the form of superstition and fetichism, but in the more cultivated it becomes a trust, not only in the order and course of nature, but in something Higher, over and above nature, something that guides, and can help without "*interfering*."

The history of the doctrine and use of final causes is instructive. The scholastic Philosophy took note only of First and final causes. Modern Science has been much occupied with the consideration of second causes. It has claimed to be able to get along without a First Cause—"the hypothesis of a God" as scientists have called it, and has stoutly protested against the recognition of any final causes. Final causes imply an intelligent Personal agent. They account for phenomena by referring to His will, and the purpose he had in ordaining the phenomena. But strangely enough, the last evolution and final outcome of this atheistic philosophy of nature, finds itself obliged to recognize final causes, under another name perhaps, as one of the indispensable elements of its explanation of the phenomena of life and living things. In Darwin's theory of "*Natural Selection*," and "*The Struggle for Life, with Survival of the Fittest*," it becomes incumbent on him to show how and why each feature that has been produced by his process is the fittest, or makes its possessor the fittest to survive. But the very word "fittest" implies an end. a "*final cause*"—a something to or for which it is "fittest." And the recognition of this final cause becomes indispensable as a part of his explanation, and a means to it. The most forcible objections to the theory, have come from such cases as the sting of the bee, the rattle of the snake, etc. This last especially, is quite a stumbling block to the advocates of this theory. They can show no final cause for it, no reason or way in which it makes its possessor more fit or likely to survive in the struggle for life, than if he had it not. It appears to be a hindrance to him rather. It looks, as we are at present informed, and according to the best knowledge we have at our command, as though it had been designed by some wise Providence, for no special use to the snake, but rather in mercy, and with a benevolent design to man and animals, so that the snake could do them no harm without first giving a warning to his victim.

The effort to escape this difficulty has led to the suggestion of a correlation of parts and properties, such that two or more, are or may be so united that the one cannot come without the other; and while the one is good for the animal, the other is bad, and yet on the whole, the usefulness of the useful one predominates over the hindrance of the other. Doubtless there is such a connection in some cases. There is inconvenience in the weight of the elephant, but he could hardly have his size and strength without it. But after all—this hypothesis fails in many cases.

But with or without this doctrine the whole theory fails and falls to the ground without the recognition of final causes—ends and purposes for which things exist—ends and purposes that can have no reality without some one who purposed and intended them.

It is certainly and old myth, if it is not a divine record that man's earliest efforts after knowledge, was accompanied with, if they did not proceed from, a disposition to unbelief and disobedience. And from that day to this, there has been something of a natural antagonism between the two powers of mind. Hence it is not at all surprising if we find those who are constitutionally least inclined to believe and obey, making themselves most conspicuous among those who engage in the pursuit of science.

But there is more in the soul than intellect—more in life than merely to know. Poetry and Religion are necessary as well as Science. Man is not satisfied with facts and laws alone. They are dry and hard—and in the language of the old heathen Epicurus, "inexorable." Whereas man wants something that is glowing with life; something that kindles imagination; something that inspires hope, even "the hope," which as Epicurus has said "comes only from prayer and the worship of God."

I like to repeat the words of this old philosopher. For heathen, sensualist, and materialist though he were, I have scarcely found anything in all my researches, preparatory to writing these Lectures, that pleased me more. Buddha is reported as having said, "All of you who are in doubt, whether there is a future life, had better believe there is one; you will then abandon sin and act virtuously, and if there should be no result, such a life will bring a good name and the regard of men." It seems to me, however, that the Greek philosopher, living some three hundred years later, puts the matter still more pointedly, when he says, "Wherefore it is better to follow that which is told us of the gods, than to be slaves to fate, which is all that the physical sciences can present us; for the former

gives us a hope that comes of prayer and the worship of God, but the latter leave us to the necessity which is inexorable." And yet, we have, as I think, a more sure Word of prophecy, which says unto us, "Come unto Me, all ye that labor and are heavy laden, and I will give you rest. Take my yoke upon you and learn of me; for I am meek and lowly in heart, and ye shall find rest unto your souls. For my yoke is easy and my burden is light."

And thus I bring to their Conclusion, my Lectures on the History of Philosophy. My plan has differed from that of others, as you must have noticed, in that I have given the opinions of the philosophers *in their own words* quoted at length; giving you the best translation I could make when I felt competent to make a translation, and when I did not I have given you one that was made by a friendly hand. I have also given you, along with the history of speculative opinions an account of the progress of the Natural Sciences and of Pure Mathematics as well.

The History of Philosophy, however, is but one Chapter in the broader and more comprehensive subject, the Philosophy of History. We see man beginning his career in an unreasoning, unquestioning belief and awe, an "unconscious monotheism" as Max Müller calls it. We see this with the eastern Aryans—the Hindoos—developing into a pantheism, while with the more active Aryans of the West, as the Greeks, it becomes a polytheism. With the Mongolic and Shemitic races it takes the form of a monotheistic personalism, with superstition, fetichism and idolatry prevailing everywhere. Philosophy came in afterward and began in scepticism and distrust of the prevailing theories and myths—seeking to establish Science in the place of mere unreasoning credulity; and with this scepticism there came the relaxation of restraint, and something of a disregard of the inevitable consequence of wrong doing.

But by the processes of investigation and analysis, the pursuit of science itself brings us back to the original starting point—not now, indeed, an "*unconscious* monotheism," but a theism, consciously held and based on most impregnable foundations, which asserts the existence of One God,—before all, over all, and in all; Whose ways are in His works, and Whose will is seen in the course of his Providence, in the History of the World, and in the experience of each human heart. A God, near and yet far off—known by all, and yet comprehended by none—a God whose presence is law, and order, and peace, and Whose fruition is eternal life and Heaven. And in the course of this evolution, the two, science and religion must again unite and be in harmony; Religion, accepting every truth and fact of science, as a part of the divine administration; and Science recognizing the truths of revelation as its necessary complement and crowning glory.

SCIENTIFIC WORKS

PUBLISHED BY

D. APPLETON & CO.

BAIN, ALEXANDER. Logic Deductive and Inductive. Rev'sd 1 vol. $2 00

——Mental Science; a Compendium of Psychology and History of Philosophy. 1 vol. 1 50

——Mind and Body. The Theories of their Relations, 1 50

——Moral Science: A Compendium of Ethics. 1 vol. 1 50

——The Senses and the Intellect. 3d edition. 1 vol. 5 00

——The Emotions and the Will. 1 vol 5 00

BANCROFT. The Native Races of the Pacific States of North America. By H. H. Bancroft. 5 vols. each 5 50

BASTIAN, H. CHARLTON, M. D., F. R. S. The Beginnings of Life: being some Account of the Nature, Modes of Origin, and Transformation of Lower Organisms. 2 vols. 5 00

——Diseases of Nerves and Spinal Cord. (In press.)

——On Paralysis from Brain Disease in its Common Forms, 1 75

BECKER, (BERNARD H.) Scientific London, 1 75

BIXBY, J. T. Similarities of Physical and Religious Knowledge, 1 v. 1 50

BUCKLEY, A. B. The Progress of Science. A Short History of Natural Science, and the Progress of Discovery, for Scholars and Young Persons. 1 vol. 2 00

CAZELLES Dr. M. F. Outline of the Evolution Philosophy. Translated from the French. 1 vol. 1 00

CLARK'S Mind in Nature; or the Origin of Life and the Mode of Development in Animals. 200 Illustrations. 1 vol. 3 50

DARWIN'S Origin of Species by Means of Natural Selection. New and revised edition. By Charles Darwin, M. A., F. R. S., F. G. S.; with copious index. 1 vol. 2 00

——Descent of Man; and Selection in Relation to Sex. With many Illustrations. A new edition. 1 vol. 3 00

——Journal of Researches into the Natural History and Geology of the Countries visited during the Voyage of H. M. S. Beagle around the World. 1 vol. 2 00

——Emotional Expressions of Man and the Lower Animals, 3 50

DARWIN, The 4 vols., uniform, Cl., 10 50

——The Variation of Animals and Plants under Domestication. 2 vols Illustrated 5 00

——Insectivorous Plants. 2 00

——The Movements and Habits of Climbing Plants. Second edition, revised. Illustrated. 1 vol. 1 25

——On the Results of Cross and Self Fertilization in the Vegetable Kingdom, 2 00

ENNIS, JACOB. The Origin of the Stars and the Causes of their Motions and their Light. 1 vol. 2 00

EVANS. The Ancient Stone Implements, Weapons and Ornaments of Great Britain. By John Evans, F. R. S., F. S. A. Illust'd. 1 vol. 5 00

FONTAINE, EDWARD. How the World was Peopled. Ethnological Lectures by Rev. Edward Fontaine, Professor of Theology and Natural Science. 1 vol. 2 00

GALTON, FRANCIS, F. R. S. Hereditary Genius: An Inquiry into its Laws and Consequences. 1 vol. 2 00

GEIKIE, JAS. The Great Ice Age, and its Relation to the Antiquity of Man. By James Geikie, F. R. S. E. F. G. S. Maps and illus. 1 vol. 2 50

HAECKEL. The History of Creation; or, the Development of the Earth and its Inhabitants by the Action of Natural Causes. From the German of Ernst Haeckel, Professor in the University of Jena. Lithographic Plates. In 2 vols. 5 00

HARRIS GEORGE, F. S. A. Civilization considered as a Science. 1 v. 1 50

HELMHOLTZ, H. Profess r of Physics in the University of Berlin. Trans'ated by E. Atkinson, Ph. D. F. C. S. ... 2 00

HUXLEY'S Man's Place in Natnre. 1 vol ... 1 25
——On the Origin of Species. 1 vol. 1 00
——More Criticisms on Darwin, and Administrative Nihilism. 1 vol... 50
——A Manual of the Anatomy of Vertebrated Animals. Illus. 1 vol. 2 50
——Lay Sermons, Addresses and Reviews. 1 vol ... 1 75
——Critiques and Addresses ... 1 50
——Direct Evidence of Evolution. In press ...

HUXLEY & YOUMANS'S Elements of Physiology and Hygiene. By T. Huxley and W. J. Youmans. 1 v. 1 50

INTERNATIONAL SCIENTIFIC SERIES.

No. I. Forms of Water in Clouds, Rain, Rivers, Ice, and Glaciers. By Prof. John Tyndall, LL. D., F. R. S. 1 vol ... 1 50

II. Physics and Politics; or, Thoughts on the Application of the Principle of "Natural Selection," and "Inheritance," to Political Society. By Walter Bagehot, Esq. 1 vol.... 1 50

III. Foods. By Edward Smith, M.D., LL. B., F. R. S. 1 vol ... 1 75

IV. Mind and Body. The Theories of their Relations. By Alex. Bain, LL. D., Professor of Logic in the University of Aberdeen, 1 vol.... 1 50

V. The Study of Sociology. By Herbert Spencer. 1 vol ... 1 50

VI. The New Chemistry. By Prof. Josiah P. Cooke, Jr., of Harvard University. 1 vol ... 2 00

VII. The Conservation of Energy. By Prof. Balfour Stewart, LL. D., F. R. S. 1 vol ... 1 50

VIII. Animal Locomotion; or, Walking, Swimming and Flying, with a Dissertation on Aeronautics. By J. Bell Pettigrew, M. D., F. R. S. 1 vol. Illustrated ... 1 75

IX. Responsibility in Mental Disease. By Henry Maudsley, M. D. 1 vol. 1 50

X. The Science of Law. By Prof. Sheldon Amos. 1 vol ... 1 75

XI. Animal Mechanism. A Treatise on Terrestrial and Aerial Locomotion. By E. J. Marey. Illustrated 1 75

XII. The History of the Conflict between Religion and Science. By John Wm. Draper, M. D., LL. D.... 1 75

XIII. The Theory of Descent and Darwinism. By Prof. Oscar Schmidt 1 vol ... 1 50

XIV. The Chemistry of Light and Photography. By Prof. Vogel. 1 v 2 00

XV. Fungi, their Nature and Uses. By M. C. Cooke, M. A., LL. D. 1 v. 1 50

XVI. The Life and Growth of Language; an Outline of Linguistic Science. By William Dwight Whitney, Professor of Sanskrit and Comparative Philology in Yale College. 1 vol ... 1 50

XVII. Money and the Mechanism of Exchange. By W. Stanley Jevons, M. A., F. R. S. 1 vol ... 1 75

XVIII. The Nature of Light, with a General Account of Physical Optics. By Dr. Eugene Lommel, Professor of Physics in the University of Erlangen. Illustrated, 1 vol... 2 00

XIX. Animal Parasites and Messmates. By P. J. Van Beneden. Illustrated. 1 vol ... 1 50

XX. On Fermentation. By P. Schutzenberger, Director at the Chemical Laboratory at the Sorbonne. Illustrated. 1 vol ... 1 50

XXI. The Five Senses of Man. By Prof. Bernstein, of the University of Halle. 1 vol ... 1 75

XXII. The Theory of Sound in its Relation to Music. By Prof. Pietro Blaserna, of the Royal University of Rome. 1 vol ... 1 50

Others in preparation.

LE CONTE, Prof. JOSEPH. Religion and Science. A Series of Sunday Lectures on the Relation of Natural and Revealed Religion. By Joseph Le Conte, Prof. of Nat. Hist. in the Univ. of Califoania. 1v 1 50

LUBBOCK, Sir JOHN. Origin of Civilization, and the Primitive Condition of Man. By Sir John Lubbock, Bart., M. P. 1 vol ... 2 00
——Prehistoric Times. Illus. 1 vol. 5 00

LYELL'S Principles of Geology. Illustrated. A new revised edition. 2 vols ... 8 00
——Elements of Geology. Sixth edition, greatly enlarged. Illus. 1 v. 3 50

MAUDSLEY, HENRY. Body and Mind; an Inquiry into their Connection and Mutual Influence, specially in reference to Mental Disorders. Revised edition. By Henry Maudsley, M. D. 1 vol.... 1 50

MIND: A Quarterly Review of Psychology and Philosophy. Nos. 1, 2, and 3, now ready, 1876. Pr year, 4 00

Pr Number 1 00

MIVART, ST. GEO. On the Genesis of Species. By St. Geo. Mivart, F. R. S. Illustrated................ 1 75

—Man and Apes. An Exposition of Structural Resemblances and Differences. 1 vol................ 1 50

—Lessons from Nature, as manifested in Mind and Matter. 1 vol.. 2 00

— Contemporary Evolution. An Essay on Recent Social Changes. 1 vol............................ 1 50

ORMATHWAITE, LORD. Astronomy and Geology compared,....... 1 00

PAPILLON, FERNAND. Nature and Life. Facts and Doctrines relating to the Constitution of Matter, the New Dynamics, and the Philosophy of Nature. By Fernand Papillon. Transl. from the French. 1 vol............................ 2 00

POPULAR SCIENCE MONTHLY, The Edited by E. L. Youmans. Vols. I, II, III, IV, V, VI, VII, VIII, and IX, now ready. Per volume, ... 3 50 Terms, $5 per annum, or 50 cents per copy.

POPULAR SCIENCE LIBRARY, pr volume,....................... 1 00

Health. By Dr. Edward Smith, F. R. S.

The Natural History of Man. By Professor A. de Quatrefages. Translated from the French.

The Science of Music. By Sedley Taylor.

Outline of the Evolution Philosophy. By Dr. E. Cazelles. Translated from the French.

English Men of Science, Their Nature and Nurture. By F. Galton, F. R. S.

PROCTOR, R. A. Other Worlds than Ours. By R. A. Proctor, B. A., F. R. A. S. Illustrated........... 2 50

— Light science for Leisure Hours. A series of Familiar Essays on Scientific Subjects,...... .... 1 75

— Essays on Astronomy. A Series of Papers on Planets and Meteors the Sun, Stars, etc. 1 vol........ 4 50

—The Moon, her Motions, Aspect, Scenery, and Physical Conditions. With Three Lunar Photographs, and many Plates, Charts, etc., 1 v. 5 00

— The Expanse of Heaven. A Series of Essays on the Wonders of the Firmament. 1 vol............ 2 00

— Our Place among Infinities. A Series of Essays contrasting our Little Abode in Space and Time with the Infinities around us. 1 v. 1 75

RIBOT, TH. Heredity; a Psychological Study on its Phenomena. 1 v. 2 00

— English Psychology. Translated from the French of Th. Ribot. 1 vol................................ 1 50

ROSCOE, HENRY E. Spectrum Analysis. By Henry E. Roscoe, B.A., Ph. D., F. R. S. With illustrations. 1 vol................................ 9 00

SCHELLEN, H. Spectrum Analysis in its Application to Terrestrial Substances, and the Physical Constitution of the Heavenly Bodies. Familiarly explained by Dr. H. Schellen, Director der Realschule I. O. Cologne. Translated from the German. With Wood cuts, colored plates and Maps. 1 vol......... 6 00

SCIENCE PRIMERS:

1. Introductory. By Prof. Huxley, F. R. S. In Press.
2. Chemistry. By Prof. Roscoe... 45
3. Physics. By Balfour Stewart. With Illustrations,................ 45
4. Physical Geography. By Archibald Geikie, LL. D., F. R. S.,...... 45
5. Geology. By Archibald Geikie, LL. D., F. R. S................ 45
6. Physiology. By M. Foster, M. A., M. D., F. R. S................ 45
7. Astronomy. By J. Norman Lockyer, F. R. S 45
8. Botany. By Dr. J. D. Hooker.... 45

Others in preparation.

SPENCER, HERBERT. Education, Intellectual, Moral, and Physical.. 1 25

—First Principles.................. 2 50

—Essays; Moral, Political, and Æsthetic. 1 vol...................... 2 50

—Illustrations of Universal Progress. A Selection of his Best Papers. 1 vol..................... 2 50

——Social Statics; or, the Conditions essential to Human Happiness specified. 1 vol.................. 2 50

——The Principles of Biology. 2 vols 5 00

——The Principles of Psychology. 2 vols............................ 5 00

——Philosophy of Style............. 50

—— Recent Discussions in Science, Philosophy, and Morals. New edition.............................. 2 00

——Works. 10 vols................ 44 00

——Sociology. 1 vol............... 1 50

——DISCRIPTIVE SOCIOLOGY, or Groups of Sociological Facts, classified and arranged by Herbert Spencer. To be published in Parts, folio, boards. To subscribers, for the whole work, per part... ...... 3 50
Single Parts..................... 4 00

NOW READY:

No. 1. Division III., Part I. C. ENGLISH. Compiled and abstracted by James Cullier.

No. 2, Division II., Part I. B. Ancient Mexicans, Central Americans, Chibehos, and Ancient Peruvians. Compiled and abs racted by Lichard Scheppig, Ph. D.

No. 3, Division I., Part I. A. Types of the Lowest Races. Negritto Races. Malayo-Polynesian Races. Compiled and abstracted by Prof. David Duncan.

No. 4, Division I, Part II, A. African Races. Compiled and abstracted by Prof. David Duncan.

The balance of the work in active preparation.

——Principles of Sociology. Issued in Quarterly Numbers of eighty pages each. Subscription, per annum............................... 2 00

TYNDALL, Prof. JOHN. Heat as a Mode of Motion. 1 vol........... 2 00

——On Sound: A Course of Eight Lectures. By John Tyndall, LL. D., F. R. S. Illustrated. 1 vol.... 2 00

——Fragments of Science for Unscientific People..................... 2 50

——Light and Electricity............ 1 25

——Hours of Exercise in the Alps. With Illustrations................ 2 00

——Faraday as a Discoverer. A Memoir. 1 vol....................... 1 00

——On Forms of Water............ 1 50

——Radiant Heat.................. 5 00

——Six Lectures on Light. With an Appendix and numerous Illustrations.......................Paper, 75

—— Banquet. Proceedings at. Given at Delmonico's, New York, February 4, 1873, paper,.............. 50

—— Address delivered before the British Association, assembled at Belfast. Revised. 1 vol......... 50

YOUMANS, E. L. Class-Book of Chemistry. New edition,........ 1 50

—— Hand-Book of Household Science,............................ 1 50

—— The Culture demanded by Modern Life: A Series of Addresses and Arguments on the Claims of Scientific Education. Edited by Edward L. Youmans, M. D. 1 vol. 2 00

—— Correlation and Conservation of Forces. A Series of Expositions by Prof. Grove, Prof. Helmholtz, Dr. Mayer, Dr. Faraday, Prof. Liebig, and Dr. Carpenter. Edited by Edward L. Youmans, M. D. 1 vol................................ 2 00

NEW BOOKS.

BAGEHOT, WALTER. The English Constitution, and other Political Essays. Latest Revised edition. 1 vol.............................. 2 00

TYNDALL, JOHN. Lessons in Electricity, at the Royal Institution, 1875–'6. 1 vol.................. 1 00

——Fragments of Science. A Series of Detached Essays. Revised and enlarged edition. 1 vol........... 2 50

DARWIN, CHARLES. The various Contrivances by which Orchids are fertilized by Insects. Revised with illustrations. 1 vol................ 1 75

—— The Effects of Cross and Self fertilization in the Vegetable Kingdom. 1 vol....................... 2 00

www.ingramcontent.com/pod-product-compliance
Lightning Source LLC
LaVergne TN
LVHW021358110826
845150LV00007B/1704

* 9 7 8 1 4 2 5 5 1 2 8 7 3 *